Ann Ward Radcliffe

A Journey Through Holland and Germany

Ann Ward Radcliffe

A Journey Through Holland and Germany

ISBN/EAN: 9783743373068

Manufactured in Europe, USA, Canada, Australia, Japa

Cover: Foto ©Andreas Hilbeck / pixelio.de

Manufactured and distributed by brebook publishing software (www.brebook.com)

Ann Ward Radcliffe

A Journey Through Holland and Germany

A

JOURNEY

THROUGH

HOLLAND, &c.

MADE IN THE SUMMER OF 1794.

THE Author begs leave to obferve, in explanation of the ufe made of the plural term in the following pages, that, her journey having been performed in the company of her neareft relative and friend, the account of it has been written fo much from their mutual obfervation, that there would be a deception in permitting the book to appear, without fome acknowledgement, which may diftinguifh it from works entirely her own. The title page would, therefore, have contained the joint names of her hufband and herfelf, if this mode of appearing before the Public, befides being thought by that relative a greater acknowledgement than was due to his fhare of the work, had not feemed liable to the imputation of a defign to attract attention by extraordinary novelty. It is, however, neceffary to her own fatisfaction, that fome notice fhould be taken of this affiftance. She may, therefore, be permitted to intrude

a few

a few more words, as to this subject, by saying, that where the œconomical and political conditions of countries are touched upon in the following work, the remarks are less her own than elsewhere.

With respect to the book itself, it is, of course, impossible, and would be degrading if it were not so, to prevent just censure by apologies; and unjust censure she has no reason, from her experience, to fear; —but she will venture to defend a practice adopted in the following pages, that has been sometimes blamed for its apparent nationality, by writers of the most respectable authority. The references to England, which frequently occur during the foreign part of the tour, are made because it has seemed that one of the best modes of describing to any class of readers what they may not know, is by comparing it with what they do.

May 20, 1795.

JOURNEY, &c.

HELVOETSLUYS.

About twenty hours after our embarkation, at Harwich, and six after our first sight of the low-spread and barren coast of *Goree*, we reached this place, which is seated on one of many inlets, that carry the waters of the German Ocean through the southern part of the province of Holland. *Goree*, rendered an island by these

these encroachments of the sea, is always the first land expected by the seamen; or rather they look out for the lofty tower of its church, which, though several miles more distant than the shore, is visible when that cannot be discerned. The entrance of the water between the land, in a channel probably three leagues wide, soon after commences; and Helvoetsluys is then presently seen, with the masts of vessels rising above its low houses, amidst green embankments and pastures, that there begin to reward the care of excluding the sea.

The names of Dutch towns are in themselves expressive of the objects most interesting to a people, who, for opportunities of commerce, have increased their original and natural dangers, by admitting the water in some parts, while, for their homes and their lives, they must prevent it from encroaching upon others. *Dam*, *Sluice*, or *Dyke* occur in almost all their compounded titles. The sluice,

sluice, which gives this town part of its name, is also its harbour; affording, perhaps, an outlet to the overflowings of the country behind, but filled at the entrance to the depth of more than eighty feet by the sea, with which it communicates.

Upon the banks of this sluice, which are partly artificial, the town is built in one short street of small houses, inhabited chiefly by tradesmen and innkeepers. The dockyard bounds the sluice and the town, communicating with the former by gates, over which a small pivot bridge connects the two sides of the street. Each head of the pier, or harbour, has been extended beyond the land, for several yards by pile work, filled with earth and large stones, over which there is no pavement, that its condition may be constantly known. We stepped from the packet upon one of these, and, walking along the beams, that pass between the immense piles, saw how closely the *interstices* were filled, and how the earth and stones were again compacted by a strong kind of basket-work.

The arrival of a packet is the chief incident known at Helvoetsluys; and, as ours entered the harbour about noon, and in fine weather, perhaps, a fourth part of the inhabitants were collected as spectators. Their appearance did not surprise us with all the novelty, which we had expected from the first sight of a foreign people. The Dutch seamen every where retain the national dress; but the other men of Helvoetsluys differ from Englishmen in their appearance chiefly by wearing coarser clothes, and by bringing their pipes with them into the street. Further on, several women were collected about their baskets of herbs, and their dress had some of the novelty, for which we were looking; they had hats of the size of a small chinese umbrella, and almost as gaudily lined within;

within; clofe, white jackets, with long flaps; fhort, coloured petticoats, in the fhape of a diving bell; yellow flippers, without quarters at the heel; and caps, that exactly fitted the head and concealed the hair, but which were ornamented at the temples by gold filiagree clafps, twirling, like vine tendrils, over the cheeks of the wearer.

Our inn was kept by Englifh people, but the furniture was entirely Dutch. Two beds, like cribs in a fhip, were let into the wainfcot; and we were told, that, in all the inns on our journey, we fhould feldom, or never, be fhewn into a room, which had not a bed.

Helvoetfluys, it fufficiently appears, is a very inconfiderable place, as to its fize and inhabitants. But it is not fo in naval, or military eftimation. It is diftant about ten or twelve miles from the open fea, yet is nearly fecure from attack on this fide, becaufe that part of the approach, which is deep enough for large veſſels, is commanded by batteries on ſhore. It ſtands in the middle of an immenſe bay, large enough to contain all the navy of Holland, and has a dockyard and arſenal in the centre of the fortifications. When we paſſed through it, ſix ſhips of the line and two frigates were lying in the dockyard, and two ſhips of the line and three frigates, under the command of an Admiral, in the bay.

The fortifications, we were aſſured upon good military authority, were in ſuch repair, that not a ſod was out of its place, and are ſtrong enough to be defended by five thouſand men againſt an hundred thouſand, for five weeks. The ſea water riſes to a conſiderable height in a wide ditch, which ſurrounds them. We omitted to copy an inſcription, placed on one of the walls, which told the date of their completion; but this was

was probably about the year 1696, when the harbour was perfected. Though the dockyard can be only one of the dependencies upon that of Rotterdam, the largeſt ſhips of that juriſdiction are preſerved here, on account of the convenient communication between the port and the ſea.

Near this place may be obſerved, what we examined with more leiſure upon our return, the ingenuity, utility and vaſtneſs of the embankments, oppoſed by the Dutch to the ſea. From Helvoetſluys eaſtward, for many miles, the land is preſerved from the ſea only by an artificial mound of earth, againſt which the water heavily and often impetuouſly ſtrives for admiſſion into the ſheltered plains below. The ſea, at high water, is ſo much above the level of the ground, from which it is thus boldly ſeparated, that one who ſtands on the land ſide of the embankment hears the water foaming, as if over his head. Yet the mound itself, which has stood for two centuries, at least, without repair, though with many renewals of the means, that protect it, is still unhurt and undiminished, and may yet see generations of those, whom it defends, rising and passing away, on one side, like the fluctuations of the tides, which assail and retire from it, on the other.

It is better, however, to describe than to praise. The mound, which appears to be throughout of the same height, as to the sea, is sometimes more and sometimes less raised above the fields; for, where the natural level of the land assists in resistance to the water, the Hollanders have, of course, availed themselves of it, to exert the less of their art and their labour. It is, perhaps, for the most part, thirty feet above the adjoining land. The width at top is enough to permit the passage of two carriages, and
there

there is a fort of imperfect road along it. In its defcent, the breadth increafes fo much, that it is not very difficult to walk down either fide. We could not meafure it, and may therefore be excufed for relating how its fize may be guefled.

On the land fide, it is faid to be ftrengthened by ftone and timber, which we did not fee, but which may be there, covered by earth and grafs. Towards the fea, fomewhat above and confiderably below high-water mark, a ftrong matting of flags prevents the furge from carrying away the furface of the mound; and this is the defence which has fo long preferved it. The matting is held to the fhore by bandages of twifted flags, running horizontally, at the diftance of three or four yards from each other, and ftaked to the ground by ftrong wooden pins. As this matting is worn by every tide, a furvey of it is frequently made, and many parts appear

appear to have been just repaired. Further in the sea, it is held down by stones; above, there are posts at every forty yards, which are numbered, that the spot may be exactly described where repairs are necessary. The impost for the maintenance of these banks amounts to nearly as much as the land-tax; and, as the land could not be possessed without it, this tax has the valuable character of being occasioned by no mismanagement, and of producing no discontent.

ROTTER-

ROTTERDAM.

From Helvoetsluys to this place the usual way is by the Brill and Maesland sluice, with several changes of carriages and boats; but, on the days of the arrival of mails, a Rotterdam skipper, whose vessel has been left at a hamlet on the Maese, takes his party in carriages acrofs the island of Voorn, on which Helvoetsluys stands, to his schuyt, and from thence by the Maese to Rotterdam. We paid two ducats, or about seventeen shillings, for the whole, and found this the highest price given for travelling in Holland. Our carriage was a sort of small coach of the fashion, exhibited in paintings of the sixteenth century, but open before, and so ill-furnished with springs, that the Dutch name,

name, "a covered waggon," was not an improper description of it. A bad road led us through some meadows of meagre grass, and through fields in which corn was higher, though thinner, than in England. The prospect was over an entire level to the horizon, except that the spires of distant villages, some small clusters of trees, and now and then a wind-mill, varied it. As we approached any of these clusters, we found usually a neat farm-house sheltered within, and included, together with its garden and orchard, in a perfect green fence: the fields were elsewhere separated from each other and from the road, neither by hedges or walls, but by deep ditches filled with water, over which are laid small bridges, that may be opened in the middle by a sort of trapdoor, raised and locked to a post, to prevent the intrusion of strangers.

On the way we passed now and then a waggon

waggon filled with large brafs jugs, bright as new gold. In thefe veffels, which have fhort narrow necks, covered with a wooden ftopper, milk is brought from the field throughout Holland. It is always carried to the towns in light waggons, or carts, drawn frequently by horfes as fleek and well-conditioned as thofe in our beft coaches.

The hamlet, at which we were to embark, was bufied in celebrating fome holiday. At the only cottage, that had a fign, we applied for refrefhment, partly for the purpofe of feeing its infide, by which we were not a little gratified. Thirty or forty peafants were feated upon benches, about a circle, in which children were dancing to the fcraping of a French fiddler. The women wore their large hats, fet up in the air like a fpread fan, and lined with damafk, or flowered linen. Children of feven years old, as well as women of feventy, were in this prepofte-
rous

rous disguise. All had necklaces, ear-rings, and ornamental clasps for the temples, of solid gold: some wore large black patches of the size of a shilling. The old woman of the house had a valuable necklace and head-dress. Among the group were many of Teniers' beauties; and over the countenances of the whole assemblage was an air of modesty, decorum, and tranquillity. The children left their dancing, to see us; and we had almost lost our tide to Rotterdam, by staying to see them.

Our sail up the Maese was very delightful. The river flows here with great dignity, and is animated with vessels of all countries passing to and from Rotterdam. The huge Archangelman, the lighter American, the smart, swift Englishman, and the bulky Dutchman, exhibit a various scene of shipping, upon a noble surface of water, winding between green pastures and rich villages,

spread

spread along the low shores, where pointed roofs, trees, and masts of fishing-boats, are seen mingled in striking confusion. Small trading schuyts, as stout and as round as their masters, glided by us, with crews reposing under their deep orange sails, and frequently exchanging some salute with our captain. On our left, we passed the little town of Flaarding, celebrated for its share of the herring-fishery on our coasts; and Schiedam, a larger port, where what is called the Rotterdam geneva is made, and where several English vessels were visible in the chief street of the place. After a sail of two hours we distinguished Rotterdam, surrounded by more wood than had yet appeared, and overtopped by the heavy round tower of the great church of St. Lawrence. The flatness of its situation did not allow us here to judge of its extent; but we soon perceived the grandeur of an ample city, extending

tending along the north fhore of the Maefe, that, now fpreading into a noble bay, along the margin of which Rotterdam rifes, fweeps towards the fouth-eaft.

The part of the city firft feen, from the river, is faid to be among the fineft in Europe for magnificence and convenience of fituation. It is called the *Boom Quay, i. e.* the quay with trees, having rows of lofty elms upon the broad terrace, that fupports many noble houfes, but which is called a quay, becaufe fhips of confiderable burthen may moor againft it, and deliver their cargoes. The merchants accordingly, who have refidences here, have their warehoufes adjoining their houfes, and frequently build them in the form of domeftic offices. The quay is faid to be a mile in length, but appears to be fomewhat lefs. There are houfes upon it, as handfome as any in the fquares of London.

At the top of the *Boom Quay* is one of the *Heads*, or entrances by water into the city, through which the greater part of its numerous canals receive their supplies. On the approach to it, the view further up the Maese detains attention to the bank of this noble river. A vast building, erected for the Admiralty, is made, by a bend of the Maese, almost to face you; and the interval, of more than a quarter of a mile, is filled by a line of houses, that open directly, and without a terrace, upon the water. The fronts of these are in another street; but they all exhibit, even on this side, what is the distinction of Dutch houses and towns, a nicety and a perfectness of preservation, which give them an air of gaiety without, and present you with an idea of comfort within. What in England would be thought a symptom of extraordinary wealth, or extravagance, is here universal. The outside of every house, however old or humble, is as clean

clean as water and paint can make it. The window-shutters are usually coloured green; and whatever wood appears, whether in cornices or worse ornaments, is so frequently cleaned, as well as painted, that it has always the gloss of newness. Grotesque ornaments are sometimes by these means rendered conspicuous; and a street acquires the air of a town in a toyshop; but in general there is not in this respect such a want of taste as can much diminish the value of their care.

Our skipper reached his birth, which is constantly in the same place, soon after passing the *Head*, and entering by a canal into one of the principal streets of the city. Between the broad terraces of this street, which are edged with thick elms, the innumerable masts of Dutch schuyts, with gay pendants and gilded tops; the hulls of larger vessels from all parts of the world; the white drawbridges, covered with passengers; the boats,

HOLLAND.

continually moving, without noise or apparent difficulty; all this did somewhat surprise us, who had supposed that a city so familiarly known, and yet so little mentioned as Rotterdam, could have nothing so remarkable as its wealth and trade.

In our way from the boat to the inn, other fine canals opened upon us on each side, and we looked at them till we had lost the man, whom we should have followed with our baggage. We had no fear that it would be stolen, knowing the infrequency of robberies in Holland; and the first person, of whom we could enquire our way in broken Dutch, acknowledged his country people by answering in very good English. There are many hundreds of British residents in this place, and our language and commerce have greatly the sway here over those of all other foreign nations. The Dutch inscriptions over warehouses and shops have frequently English translations underneath them. Of

large

large veffels, there are nearly as many Englifh as Dutch in the harbour; and, if you fpeak to any Dutchman in the ftreet, it is more probable that he can anfwer in Englifh than in French. On a Sunday, the Englifh fill two churches, one of which we attended on our return. It is an ob-. long brick building, permitted by the States to be within the jurifdiction of the Bifhop of London, Parliament having given 2500l. towards its completion in the beginning of the prefent century. There are alfo many Proteftant diffenters here, who are faid to have their offices of worfhip performed with the ability, fimplicity, and zeal, which are ufually to be obferved in the devotions of that clafs of Chriftians.

Rotterdam is the fecond city for fize, and perhaps the firft for beauty, in the United Provinces; yet, when we walked through it the next day, and expected to find the magnificence of the approach equalled in its interior,

interior, we were compelled to withdraw a little of the premature admiration, that had begun to extend to the whole place. The ſtreet, where there is moſt trade and the greateſt paſſage, the *Hoogſtraat*, is little wider, though it is abundantly cleaner, than a London lane. The Stadthouſe is in this ſtreet, and is an old brick building, with a peaked roof, not entirely free from fantaſtic ornament. It has been built too early to have the advantages of modern elegance, and too late for the ſanction of ancient dignity. The market-place has only one wide acceſs; and the communication between the ſtreet, from the principal *Head*, and that in which the Exchange is placed, is partly through a very narrow, though a ſhort paſ-ſage. The Exchange itſelf is a plain ſtone building, well deſigned for its purpoſe, and completed about fifty years ago. The happieſt circumſtance relating to it is, that the merchants are numerous enough to fill the

colonnades

colonnades on the four sides of its interior. Commerce, which cannot now be long discouraged in any part of Europe, because without it the interest of public debts cannot be paid, is the permanent defender of freedom and knowledge against military glory and politics.

From the Exchange there is an excellent walk to the market-place, where the well-known statue of ERASMUS is raised. Being represented in his doctor's dress, the figure can display little of the artist's skill; but the countenance has strong lines, and a physiognomist would not deny them to be expressive of the discernment and shrewdness of the original.

The market-place is really a large bridge, for a canal passes under it; but its size, and the easiness of ascent from the sides, prevent this from being immediately observed. Some of the surrounding houses have their dates marked upon glazed tiles. They were built

during

during the long war, that refcued the provinces from the Spanifh dominion; a time when it might be fuppofed that nothing would have been attended to, except the bufinefs of providing daily food, and the duty of refifting the enemy; but in which the Dutch enlarged and beautified their cities; prepared their country to become a medium of commerce, and began nearly all the meafures, which have led to their prefent extenfive profperity.

Near this place is the great church of St. LAWRENCE, which we entered, but did not find to be remarkable, except for a magnificent brafs baluftrade that croffes it at the upper end. A profufion of *achievements*, which cover the walls almoft to the top, contribute to its folemnity. In addition to the arms of the deceafed, they contain the dates of their birth and death, and are ufed inftead of infcriptions, though no names are exprefled upon them. Under the pulpit was an hour-glafs, which limits the difcourfe of the preacher: on one fide a wand, having at the end a velvet bag and a fmall bell; this is carried about, during an interval in the fervice, and every body puts fomething into it for the poor. The old beadle, who fhewed us the church, laid his hands upon us with pleafure, when he heard that we were Englifh, and Proteftants. There are three minifters to this church, with falaries of nearly two hundred pounds fterling each.

We went to our inn through the *Hoog-ftraat*, which was filled with people and carriages, but has no raifed pavement to feparate the one from the other. In all the towns which we faw, the footpath is diftinguifhed from the road only by being paved with a fort of light coloured brick. The Dutch fhops are in the fhape, which thofe of London are defcribed to have had fifty years fince, with fmall high windows, and

blocks

blocks between them and the street. Silversmiths expose their goods in small glass cupboards upon the blocks, and nearly all the trades make upon them what little shew is customary. Almost every tenth house displays the inscription *Tabak te koop*, " Tobacco to be sold." This street, having no canal, is occupied entirely by retail traders. We bought in it the Antwerp Gazette for two doights, or one farthing; strawberries, large and well coloured, at a lower price than they could be had six weeks later in England, but without flavour; and went into several booksellers' shops, expecting to have found something in Latin, or French, but could see only Dutch books. In another street a bookseller had several English volumes, and there are no doubt well filled shops, but not so numerous as that we could find any.

Over the canals, that flow through almost every street of Rotterdam, are great numbers

numbers of large drawbridges, which contribute much to the neat and gay appearance of the city; but, when these are raised, the obstruction to the passage occasions crowds on each side; and, therefore, in some of the most frequented parts, the bridges are entire and permanent, except for the breadth of three feet in the centre, where there is a plank, which opens upon hinges almost as easily as the lid of a trunk. Through this opening the masts of the small Dutch schuyts are easily conducted, but ships can pass only where there are drawbridges. The number of the former is immense; for, throughout the provinces, every village, if it is near a canal, has several schuyts, which carry away the superfluous produce of the country, and return with the manufactures, or stores of the towns. But neither their number, nor their neatness, is so remarkable as the ease and stillness, with which they traverse the city; and indeed ease and still-

ness

ness are much the characteristics of all the
efforts of Dutch industry. The noise and
agitation, usual whenever many persons are
employed together in other countries, are
unknown here. Ships are brought to their
moorings, schuyts pass each other in crowded canals, heavy burthens are raised and
cargoes removed, almost without a word,
that can be heard at twenty yards distance.

Another circumstance, rendering Dutch
towns freer from noise than others of equal
traffic, is the little use which is made of
waggons and carts, even where some sort
of land carriage must be employed. Heavy
commodities are usually carried about the
streets on sledges; and almost the greatest
noise is, when the driver of one of these,
after having delivered his load, meaning to
render himself a prodigy of frolicsomeness,
stands upon the hinder edges of his sledge,
and then, preventing himself from falling
backward

backward by his hold of the reins, is drawn rapidly through the admiring crowd.

We were long enough at Rotterdam, during three vifits, to fee how well it is provided with avenues towards the country and along the banks of the Maefe. To one of thefe the way is over the two *Heads*, or chief canals, each of which you crofs for a doight, or half a farthing, in boats that are continually paffing between the two fides. This little voyage faves a walk of about three hundred yards to the neareft bridge. The boats will hold twenty or thirty perfons, and the profit of them is very confiderable to the City government, which applies the money to public purpofes. Each boat is worked by one man, who pulls it over by a rope in about two minutes.

Many of the inhabitants have what they call garden-houfes upon thefe walks, and upon

upon a femi-circular road, which paſſes on the land ſide of the city; but the moſt wealthy have feats at greater diſtances, where they can be furrounded with grounds, and make the difplay of independent reſidences.

Upon the whole, Rotterdam has from its fituation many conveniences and delights, and from its ſtructure ſome magnificence, together with a general neatneſs; but is, for the moſt part, deficient in elegance, and its beauties have too much the air of prettineſſes. The canals are indifputably fine, crowned with lofty terraces, and deep enough to carry large veſſels into the centre of the city.

DELFT.

DELFT.

BETWEEN Rotterdam and this place we commenced our travelling in trechtfchuyts, which are too well known to need defcription. The fare is at the rate of about a penny per mile, and a trifle more hires the *roof*, which is a fmall feparate chamber, neareft to the ftern of the veffel, lighted by windows on each fide. In engaging this, you have an inftance of the accuracy of the Dutch in their minuteft tranfactions; a formal printed receipt, or ticket, is given for the few pence which it cofts, by a commiffary, who has no other bufinefs than to regulate the affairs of the trechtfchuyts at his gate of the city. We could never learn what proportion of the fare is paid as a tax to the State, but it is faid to be a confiderable

able part; and not only thefe fchuyts, but the ferries, the poft waggons, and the pilotage throughout the United States, are made contributory to the public funds.

The punctuality of the departure and arrival of the trechtfchuyts is well known, and juftifies the Dutch method of reckoning diftances, which is by hours, and not by leagues or miles. The canals being generally full to the brim, the top of the veffel is above the level of the adjoining country, and the view over it is of courfe extenfive; but the houfes and gardens, which are beft worth feeing, are almoft always upon the banks of the canal. We paffed feveral fuch in the way to Delft, towards which the Rotterdam merchants have their favourite feats; but Dutch gardens are rather to be noticed by an Englifhman as curiofities, than as luxuries. It is not only by the known ill tafte of their ornaments, but by the effects of climate and the foil, that gardens are de-
prived

prived of value, in a country, where the moisture is so disproportioned to the heat, that the verdure, though bright, has no fragrance, and the fruit, at its utmost size, scarcely any flavour.

A passage of two hours brought us to Delft, which we had expected to find a small and ill-inhabited place, knowing it to be not now occupied by any considerable trade. Our inn, we supposed, must be within a few minutes walk. We proceeded, however, through one street for half a mile, and, after some turnings, did not reach our inn, though we were led by the nearest way, in less than twenty minutes. During all this time we were upon the terraces of clear canals, amongst excellent houses, with a small intermixture of shops and some public buildings. The mingled admiration and weariness, which we felt here, for the first time, have been, however, often repeated; for if there is a necessity for saying what

is

is the next diftinction of Dutch towns, after their neatnefs, their fize muft be infifted upon. There are Dutch villages, fcarcely marked in a map, which exceed in fize fome of the county towns in England. *Maefland Sluice*, a place oppofite to the Brill, is one. And here is Delft, a place with fcarcely any other trade than confifts in the circulation of commodities from Rotterdam through fome neighbouring villages; which is not the feat of any confiderable part of the national government, and is inferior, in point of fituation, to all the furrounding towns. Delft, thus undiftinguifhed, fills a large circumference, with ftreets fo intricately thick, that we never went from our inn without lofing our way.

The *Doolen*, one of the beft inns in Holland, is a large building of the fixteenth century, raifed by the Spaniards, and firft intended to be a convent; but, having been ufed by the burghers of Delft for public purpofes, poses, during the struggle of the Provinces against Spain, it is now venerable as the scene of their councils and preparations. In the suite of large apartments, which were used by them, some of the city business is still transacted, and in these strangers are never entertained. Behind, is a bowling-green, in which the burghers to this day perform their military exercises: they were so employed when we came in; and it was pleasing to consider, that their inferiority to their ancestors, in point of martial appearance, was the result of the long internal peace secured by the exertions of the latter.

Over two arches of the building is the date of its erection, 1565, the year in which the destruction of all families, professing the Protestant religion either in France or Spain, is supposed to have been agreed upon at Bayonne between the sovereigns of the two countries, and one year preceding the first measures of confederate resistance in the

Low

Low Countries, which that and other efforts of perfecution produced. One of thefe arches communicates with the rooms fo long ufed by the burghers; and our hoftefs, an intelligent woman, accompanied us through them. The firft is ornamented with three large pictures, reprefenting feveral of the early burghers of the Commonwealth, either in arms or council. A portrait of BARNE-VELDT is marked with the date and the painter's name, " MICHAEL MIEREVELD " *delineavit ac perfunctoriè pinxit,* 1617," one year before the flagitious arreft of BARNEVELDT, in defiance of the conftitution of the provinces, by MAURICE of ORANGE. A piece, exhibiting fome of the burghers in arms, men of an handfome and heroic appearance, is alfo dated, by having 1648 painted on a drum; that, which fhews them in council, has a portrait of GROTIUS, painted when he was feventeen. His face is is the seventh from the right hand in the second row.

Beyond this room are others containing several score of small cupboards, on the doors of each of which are two or three blazonries of arms. Here are deposited some parts of the dress and arms of an association of Arquebusiers, usual in all the Dutch towns; the members of which society assemble annually in October, to shoot at a target placed in a pavilion of the old convent garden. The markſman takes his aim from the fartheſt room; and between him and the mark are two walls, perforated two feet and a half in length, and eight inches in breadth, to permit the passage of the shot. A man stands in the pavilion, to tell where the ball has struck; and every markſman, before he shoots, rings a bell, to warn this person out of the way. He that firſt hits a white spot in the target, has his liquor, for the ensuing year,

year, free of excise duty; but, to render this more difficult, a stork is suspended by the legs from a string, which, passing down the whole length of the target, is kept in continual motion by the agitation of the bird. It did not appear whether the stork has any other share in this ancient ceremony, which is represented in prints of considerable date. It is held near the ground, out of the way of the shot, and is certainly not intended to be hurt; for the Dutch have no taste for cruelty in their amusements. The stork, it is also known, is esteemed by them a sort of tutelary bird; as it once was in Rome, where ASELLUS SEMPRONIUS RUFUS, who first had them served at an entertainment, is said to have lost the Prætorship for his sacrilegious gluttony. In these trivial enquiries we passed our first evening at Delft.

Early the next morning, a battalion of regular troops was reviewed upon a small plain within the walls of the town. The uniform is blue and red; in which the Dutch officers have not quite the smart appearance of ours. One of these, who gave the word to a company, was a boy, certainly not more than fifteen, whose shrill voice was ludicrously heard between the earnest shouts of the others. The firing was very exact, which is all that we can tell of the qualities of a review.

Delft was a place of early importance in the United Provinces, being one of the six original cities, that sent Deputies to the States of the province; a privilege, which, at the instance of their glorious WILLIAM the First of ORANGE, was afterwards properly extended to twelve others, including Rotterdam and the Brill. Yet it is little celebrated for military events, being unfortified, and having probably always obeyed the fortune of the neighbouring places. The circumstance which gives it a melancholy place in history, is the murder of the wife and beneficent

ficent Prince who founded the republic. His palace, a plain brick building, is still in good repair, where strangers are always shewn the staircase on which he fell, and the holes made in the wall by the shot that killed him. The old man, who keeps the house, told the story with as much agitation and interest as if it had happened yesterday. "The Prince and Princess came out of that chamber—here stood the Prince, here stood the murderer; when the Prince stepped here to speak to him about the passport, the villain fired, and the Prince fell all along here and died. Yes, so it was—there are the holes the balls made." Over one of these, which is large enough to admit two fingers, is this inscription:

"*Hier onder staen de Teykenen der Kooglen daar meede Prins Willem van Orange is doorschootten op* 10 July, A. 1584."

To this detestable action the assassin acknowledged himself to have been instigated by by the proclamation of Philip the Second, offering a reward for its perpetration. The Princefs, who had the wretchednefs to witnefs it, had loft her father and her former hufband in the maffacre of St. Bartholomew in France, which, though contrived by Catherine and Charles the Ninth of that country, is believed to have been the confequence of their interview at Bayonne, with Ifabella, the wife of the fame Philip.

The melancholy excited on this fpot is continued by paffing from it to the tomb of WILLIAM, in the great church, called the *Nieuwe Kerk*. There the gloomy pageantry of the black efcutcheons, above a choir, filent, empty and vaft, and the withering remains of colours, won by hands long fince gone to their decay, prolong the confideration of the tranfientnefs of human worth and happinefs, which can fo eafily be deftroyed by the command, or the hand of human villainy.

This

This tomb is thought to be not exceeded by any piece of sepulchral grandeur in Europe. Standing alone, in a wide choir, it is much more conspicuous and striking than a monumental fabric raised against a wall, at the same time that its sides are so varied as to present each a new spectacle. It was begun in 1609, by order of the States General, and completed in 1621; the artist, HENDRIK DE KEYZER, receiving 28,000 florins as its price, and 2000 more as a present. The length is 20 feet, the breadth 15, and height 27. A bronze statue of the Prince, sitting in full armour, with his sword, scarf, and commander's staff, renders one side the chief; on the other is his effigy in white marble, lying at full length; and at his feet, in the same marble, the figure of the dog, which is said to have refused food from the moment of its master's death. Round the tomb, twenty-two columns of veined or black Italian marble, of the Doric order, and,

with

with bases and capitals of white marble, support a roof or canopy, ornamented with many emblems, and with the *achievements of the Prince.*

At the corners, are the statues of Religion, Liberty, Justice, and Fortitude, of which the first rests upon a piece of black marble, on which is inscribed in golden letters the name of CHRIST; and the second holds a cap, with the inscription *Aurea Libertas*. On the four sides of the canopy are the devices of the Prince, with the inscriptions JEHO-VAH.—*Je maintiendrai Piété et Justice.*—*Te Vindice, tuta Libertas.*—And, *Sævis tranquillus in Undis.*

There are many other ornaments, which give dignity or elegance to the structure, but cannot be described without tediousness. The well-known Epitaph is certainly worth transcribing:

D. O. M. et eternæ memoriæ Gulielmi Nassoviæ, supremi Auransionensium Principis,

Patr.

Patr. patriæ, qui Belgii fortunis suas posthabuit et suorum; validissimos exercitus ære plurimum privato bis confcripfit, bis induxit; ordinum aufpiciis Hifpaniæ tyrannidem propulit; veræ religionis cultum, avitas patriæ leges revocavit, reftituit; ipfam denique libertatem tantum non affertam, Mauritio Principi, paternæ virtutis hæredi filio, ftabiliendam reliquit. Herois vere pii, prudentis, invicti, quem Philip. II. Hifp. R. Europæ timor, timuit; non domuit, non terruit; fed empto percuffore fraude nefanda fuftulit; Fœderat. Belgii provinc. perenni memor. monum. fec.

" To God the beft and higheft, and to the eternal memory of William of Naffau, Sovereign Prince of Orange, the father of his country, whofe welfare he preferred to that of himfelf and his family; who, chiefly at his own expence, twice levied and introduced a powerful army; under the fanction of the States repelled the tyranny of Spain;

recovered

recovered and restored the service of true religion and the ancient laws of the country; and finally left the liberty, which he had himself asserted, to be established by his son, Prince Maurice, the heir of his father's virtues. The Confederated Belgic Provinces have erected this monument, in perpetual memory of this truly pious, prudent and unconquered Hero, whom Philip II. King of Spain, the dread of Europe, dreaded; never overcame, never terrified; but, with wicked treachery, carried off by means of an hired assassin."

The tomb of GROTIUS is in the same church, which is a stately building of brick and stone, but has nothing of the " dim religious light," that sooths the mind in Gothic structures. Upon the steeple are many small bells, the chimes rung upon which are particularly esteemed, both for tone and tune.

On the opposite side of a very large
market-

market-place is the Town-houfe, an old building, but fo frefh and fo fantaftic with paint, as to have fome refemblance to a Chinefe temple. The body is coloured with a light, or yellowifh brown, and is two ftories high to the roof, in which there are two tier of peaked windows, each under its ornament of gilded wood, carved into an awkward refemblance of fhells. Upon the front is infcribed, "*Delphenfium Curia Reparata*," and immediately over the door " *Reparata* 1761."

The *Oude Kerk,* or Old Church, is in another part of the town, and is not remarkable, except for the tombs of LEUWENHOEK, PETER HEINE and VAN TROMP. That of LEUWENHOEK has a fhort infcription, in Latin almoft as bad as that of a verfe epitaph upon GROTIUS, in the other church. He was born, it appears, in October 1632, and died in Auguft 1723. The tombs of HEINE and VAN TROMP are very handfome.

some. There are the effigies of both in white marble, and one of the victories gained by the latter is reprefented in *alto relievo*. On account of the tombs, both churches are open, during certain hours in the day; and a beadle, or, perhaps, an almfman, is placed in each, who prefents a padlocked box, into which money may be put for the poor.

In this town is the chief arfenal of the province of Holland, except that the magazine of powder is at the diftance of about a mile from it, near the canal to Rotterdam. In 1787, when the diffenfions between the STATES GENERAL and the PRINCE of ORANGE were at their height, a provincial free corps feized this arfenal, and held it for the States till the return of the PRINCE of ORANGE to the Hague, a few weeks afterwards.

Having feen what was pointed out to our notice at Delft, and learned that its extenfivenefs fiveness was owing to the refidence of a great number of retired merchants from Rotterdam, we left it in a *trechtfchuyt* for the Hague, having little other notion of it in our minds, than that it is very dull and very rich, and of a fize, for which there is no recompenfe to a ftranger, except in confidering, that its dullnefs is the reft of thofe, who have once been bufy, and that its riches are at leaft not employed in aggravating the miferies of poverty by oftentation.

THE HAGUE.

A voyage of an hour and a half brought us here over a canal well bordered by country houfes and gardens, all of which, as in other parts of Holland, have fome infcription upon their gates, to fay, that they are pleafant, or are intended for pleafure.

Fine

Fine Sight, *Pleasant Rest*, *High Delight*, or some similar inscription, is to be seen over the door of every country house, in gold letters. On our way, we looked for Ryswick, where the treaty of 1697 was signed, and saw the village, but not the palace, which, being of free stone, is mentioned as a sort of curiosity in the country. It is this palace, which is said to contain proofs of an extraordinary dispute upon questions of ceremony. The Ambassadors, sent to prepare the treaty, are related to have contended so long, concerning their rights of precedence, that the only mode of reconciling them was to make separate entrances, and to allow the Mediating Minister alone admission by the principal gate.

From the *trechtschuyt* we had a long walk to our inn, an handsome house, standing almost in the midst of palaces, and looking over a noble sheet of water, called the *Vyver*, which extends behind the *Court*, for its whole

whole length, flowing nearly to the level of the lower windows. The *Court* itfelf, a large brick building, irregular, but light and pleafant, was entirely within our view, on the left; on the right, a row of magnificent houfes, feparated from the *Vyver* by a large mall; and, in front, beyond the *Vyver*, a broad place, bordered by feveral public buildings. In this Court all the fuperior colleges of government have their chambers, and the PRINCE of ORANGE his fuite of apartments. The foffé, which furrounds it, three drawbridges and as many gates are the only fortifications of the Hague, which has been feveral times threatened with the entrance of an enemy, but has not been taken fince 1595, when the magiftrates of the then infant republic, and all the fuperior inhabitants, retired to *Delft*, leaving the ftreets to be overrun with grafs, and the place to become a defert under the eyes of its oppreffors. During the invafion of LOUIS the FOURTEENTH,

TEENTH, it efcaped the ravages of the DUKE of LUXEMBOURG's column, by the fudden diffolution of the ice, on which he had placed 9000 foot and 2000 cavalry. Yet the advice of WILLIAM the THIRD, who probably thought money better expended in ftrengthening the frontier than the interior of the country, counteracted a plan of fortification, which was then propofed, for the third or fourth time.

The Court confifts of two fquares; in the inner of which are the apartments of the STADTHOLDER, and none but himfelf and his family can enter this in carriages, or on horfeback. On the northern fide, in the firft floor, are the apartments of the STATES GENERAL, which we faw. The principal one is fpacious, as a room, but has not the air of a hall of debate. Twenty-fix chairs for the Deputies are placed on two fides of a long table: the Prefident, whofe chair is in the centre, has on his right hand, firft,

a De-

HOLLAND.

a Deputy of his own province, then three Deputies of Friesland, and two of Groningen; on his left, six Deputies of Holland; opposite to him, nearest to the head of the table, six Deputies of Guelderland, then three of Zealand, then two of Utrecht, and two of Overyssel. The STADTHOLDER, who has a place, but not a vote, has a raised chair at the upper end of the table; the Secretary is seated opposite to him, and is allowed to wear his hat, like the Deputies, during their deliberations, but must stand uncovered, behind the President, when he reads letters, or other papers. The number of Deputies is known to be indefinite; about fifty are generally returned; and those, who are present from each province, more than the number allowed at the table, place themselves below it. The walls of this room are covered with tapestry, not representing historical events, but rural scenery; the backs and seats of the chairs are of green velvet;

and

and all the furniture, though stately and in the best condition, is without the least approach to show. These apartments, and the whole of this side of the Court, were the residence of CHARLES the FIFTH, when he visited the Hague, and of the EARL of LEICESTER, when he commanded the troops lent to the Republic by ELIZABETH.

The government of the United Provinces is too well known to permit a detailed description here; but some notice may reasonably be expected of it.

The chief depositaries of the sovereignty are not the States General, but the Provincial States, of whose Deputies the former body is composed, and without whose consent they never vote upon important measures. In the States General each Province has one vote; which, with the reasons for it, may be delivered by an unlimited number of Deputies; and the first Deputy of each province presides in the States by rotation

for

for a week. In queftions relative to peace or war, alliances, taxes, coinages, and to the privileges of provinces, no meafures can be taken but by unanimous confent; upon other occafions, a majority is fufficient. No perfons holding military offices can be Deputies to the States General, which appoints and receives all ambaffadors, declares war, makes peace, and names the Greffier, or Secretary of State, and all Staff Officers.

The Provincial States are varioufly compofed, and the interior governments of the provinces varioufly formed. In the province of Holland, which contains the moft profperous part of the Republic, there are eighteen Deputies to the Provincial States, for as many towns, and one for the nobility. The Grand Penfionary prefides in this affembly, and is always one of the Deputies from it to the States General.

The Council of Deputies is compofed of ten members: nine from the towns, and one from

from the nobility. This Council, in which the Grand Penfionary alfo prefides, regulates the finances of the province, and takes cognizance of the diftribution of troops within it.

The Council, called the Council of State, is compofed, like the States General, of Deputies returned from the provinces, and appears to be to that body, in a great meafure, what the Council of Deputies is to the Provincial States, having the direction of the army and the finances.

As provincial affairs are directed by the Provincial States, fo the affairs of each town are governed by its own Senate, which alfo returns the members, if the town is entitled to fend one, to the States of the Province, and directs the vote, which that member fhall give. The Burgomafters in each town are the magiftrates charged with the police and the finances, and are ufually elected annually by the old Council, that is, by thofe who

HOLLAND.

who have been Burgomafters, or *Echevins*. Thefe latter officers have the adminiftration of civil and criminal affairs, and are, in fome places, appointed by the Stadtholder from a double number nominated to him; in others, are accepted from the recommendation of the Stadtholder. The Bailiffs prefide in the Council of Burgomafters and Echevins; and in their name profecutions are inftituted.

Of the Deputies to the States General, fome are for life, and fome for one or more years.

Such is the nicely complicated frame of this government, in which the Senates of the Towns elect the Provincial States, and the Provincial States the States General; the latter body being incapable of deciding in certain cafes, except with unanimity and with the exprefs confent of their conftituents, the Provincial States; who again cannot give that confent, except with una-

nimity

nimity and with the consent of their constituents, the Senates.

The Stadtholder, it is seen, has not directly, and in consequence of that office, any share of the legislative power; but, being a Noble of four provinces, he, of course, participates in that part of the sovereignty, which the Nobility enjoy when they send Deputies to the Provincial States. Of Zealand he is the only Noble, all the other titled families having been destroyed in the original contest with Spain; and there are no renewals or creations of titles in the United Provinces. In Guelderland, Holland, and Utrecht, he is President of the Nobles. He is Commander of all the Forces of the Republic by sea and land; and the Council of State, of which he is a member, is, in military affairs, almost entirely under his direction; he names all subaltern officers, and recommends those for higher appointments to the States General.

neral. In Guelderland, Utrecht, and Overyſſel, which are called *Provinces aux Reglemens*, becauſe, having ſubmitted to Louis the Fourteenth, in 1672, they were not re-admitted to the Union, but with ſome ſacrifice of their privileges, he appoints to offices, without the nomination of the cities; he is Governor General of the Eaſt and Weſt Indian Companies, and names all the Directors from a treble number of candidates offered by the Proprietors. His name preſides in all the courts of law; and his heart, it may be hoped, dictates in the noble right of pardoning.

This is the eſſential form of a government, which, for two centuries, has protected as great a ſhare of civil and religious liberty as has been enjoyed in any other part of Europe, refiſting equally the chances of diſſolution, contained within itſelf; and the leſs dangerous ſchemes for its deſtruction,

tion, dictated by the jealoufy of arbitrary interefts without.

Its intricacy and delicacy are eafily feen; yet, of the objections made to it on this account, more are founded on fome maxims, affumed to be univerfal, than upon the feparate confiderations due to the condition of a feparate people. How much the means of political happinefs depend, for their effect, upon the civil characters of thofe for whom they are defigned, has been very little feen, or infifted upon. It has been unnoticed, becaufe fuch enquiries have not the brilliancy, or the facility, of general fpeculations, nor can command equal attention, nor equally reward fyftems with thofe parts of their importance, that confift in the immenfity of the fphere, to which they pretend. To extend their arms is the flagitious ambition of warriors; to enlarge their fyftems is the ambition of writers, efpecially of political

HOLLAND. 59

tical writers. A jufter effort of underftanding would aim at rendering the application of principles more exact, rather than more extenfive, and would produce enquiries into the circumftances of national character and condition, that fhould regulate that application. A more modeft eftimate of human means of doing good would fhew the gradations, through which all human advances muft be made. A more fevere integrity of views would ftipulate, that the means fhould be as honeft as the end, and would ftrive to afcertain, from the moral and intellectual character of a people, the degree of political happinefs, of which they are capable; a procefs, without which projected advances become obftructions; and the philofopher begins his experiment, for the amelioration of fociety, as prematurely as the fculptor would polifh his ftatue before he had delineated the features.

Whether the conftitution of the United
Provinces

Provinces is exactly as good an one as the people are capable of enjoying, can be determined only after a much longer and abler enquiry than we could make; but it seemed proper to observe, that, in judging this question, it is not enough to discover better forms of government, without finding also some reason to believe, that the intellectual and moral condition of the people would secure the existence of those better forms. In the mean time, they, who make the enquiry, may be assured, that, under the present * government, there is a considerable degree of political liberty, though political happiness is not permitted by the present circumstances of Europe; that the general adoption of the Stadtholder's measures by the States has been unduly mentioned to shew an immoderate influence, for that, in point of fact, his measures are often rejected; that this rejection produces no public agitation, nor can

* June 1794.

HOLLAND.

those, who differ from him in opinion, be fuccefsfully reprefented as enemies to their country; that there are very few offices, which enable private perfons to become rich, at the expence of the public, fo as to have a different intereft from them; that the fober induftry and plain manners of the people prevent them from looking to political conduct of any fort as a means of improving their fortunes; that, for thefe reafons, the intricate connections between the parts of their government are lefs inconvenient than may be fuppofed, fince good meafures will not be obftructed, or bad ones fupported, for corrupt purpofes, though mifconceptions may fometimes produce nearly the fame effect; that converfation is perfectly free; and that the habit of watching the ftrength of parties, for the purpofe of joining the ftrongeft and perfecuting the weakeft, does not occupy the minds of any numerous claffes amongft them.

We

We saw no other apartments than those of the States General, the PRINCE of ORANGE being then in his own. The Princess was at a seat in Guelderland, with her daughter-in-law, the wife of the Hereditary Prince, who had been indisposed since the surprise of the Dutch troops at Menin, on the 12th of September 1793, in which affair her husband was engaged. When the officer, who brought the first accounts, which were not written, to the Hague, had related that the younger prince was wounded, the Hereditary Princess enquired, with great eagerness, concerning his brother. The officer indiscreetly replied, that he knew nothing of him; which the Princess supposed to imply, that he was dead; and she has since been somewhat an invalid.

Though the salaries enjoyed by the Prince of Orange, in consequence of his offices, are by no means considerable, he is enabled, by his patrimonial estates, to maintain some modest

modest splendour. The Court is composed of a grand master, a marshal, a grand equerry, ten chamberlains, five ladies of honour, and six gentlemen of the chamber. Ten young men, with the title of pages, are educated at the expence of the Prince, in a house adjoining his *manege*. As Captain-General, he is allowed eight adjutants, and, as Admiral, three.

We could not learn the amount of the income enjoyed by the PRINCE of ORANGE, which must, indeed, be very variable, arising chiefly from his own estates. The greater part of these are in the province of Zealand, where seventeen villages and part of the town of Breda are his property. The fortifications of several places there are said to have been chiefly erected at the expence of the Orange family. His farms in that neighbourhood suffered greatly in the campaign of 1792, and this part of his income has since been much diminished. The management

ment of his revenues, derived from poffeffions in Germany, affords employment to four or five perfons, at an Office, feparate from his ordinary Treafury; and he had eftates in the Low Countries. All this is but the wreck of a fortune, honourably diminifhed by William the Firft of Orange, in the conteft with Spain; the remembrance of whom may, perhaps, involuntarily influence one's opinion of his fucceffors.

During May, the weftern gate of the palace is ornamented, according to ancient cuftom, with garlands for each perfon of the Orange family. Chaplets, with the initials of each, in flowers, are placed under large coronets, upon green flag-ftaffs. We paffed by when they were taking thefe down, and perceived that all the ornaments could fcarcely have coft five fhillings. So humble are the Dutch notions of pageantry.

Among the offices included within the walls of the court is a printing-houfe, in which

HOLLAND.

which the STATES GENERAL and the States of Holland employ only perfons fworn to fecrecy as to the papers committed to them. It may feem ftrange to require fecrecy from thofe, whofe art is chiefly ufeful in conferring publicity; but the truth is, that many papers are printed here, which are never communicated to the public, the States employing the prefs for the fake of its cheapnefs, and confidering that any of their members, who would fhew a printed paper, would do the fame with a written one.

In a large fquare, near the court, is the cabinet of natural hiftory, of which we have not the knowledge neceffary for giving a defcription. It is arranged in fmall rooms, which are opened, at twelve o'clock, to thofe, who have applied the day before. One article, faid to be very rare, and certainly very beautiful, was an animal of the Deer fpecies, about fourteen inches high, exquifitely fhaped and marked, and believed to be at its full growth. It was brought from the coaft of Africa.

The Stadtholder's library was accidentally fhut, owing to the illnefs of the librarian. The picture gallery was open, but of paintings we have refolved to exempt our readers from any mention. The former is faid to contain eight thoufand volumes, and fourteen thoufand prints in portfolios. Among the illuminated MSS. in vellum is one, ufed by the fanguinary Catherine De Medicis and her children; and another, which belonged to Ifabella of Caftille, the grandmother of Charles the Fifth. What muft be oddly placed in a library is a fuit of armour of Francis the Firft, which was once in the cabinet of Chriftina of Sweden. Though this collection is the private property of the Prince, the librarian is permitted to lend books to perfons, known to him and likely to ufe them advantageoufly for fcience.

We

We paffed a long morning in walking through the ftreets of this place, which contain probably more magnificent houfes than can be found in the fame fpace in any city of Northern Europe. The Gränd *Voorhout* is rather, indeed, two feries of palaces than a ftreet. Between two broad carriage-ways, which pafs immediately along the fides, are feveral alleys of tall lime trees, canopying walks, firft laid out by Charles the Fifth, in 1536, and ordered to be carefully preferved, the *placard* being ftill extant, which directs the punifhment of offenders againft them. It would be tedious to mention the many fplendid buildings in this and the neighbouring ftreets. Among the moft confpicuous is the prefent refidence of the Britifh Ambaffadors, built by HUGUETAN, the celebrated banker of LOUIS the FOURTEENTH, and that of the Ruffian Minifter, which was erected by the Penfionary BARNEVELDT. But the building, which was intended

intended to exceed all others at the Hague, is the Hotel of the Prince of NASSAU WEILBOURG; who, having married the fifter of the Prince of ORANGE, bought, at an immenfe expence, eight good houfes, facing the *Voorhout*, in order to erect upon their fcite a magnificent palace. What has been already built of this is extremely fine, in the crefcent form; but a German, arriving to the expenditure of a Dutch fortune, probably did not eftimate it by Dutch prices. It was begun eighteen years fince, and, for the laft twelve, has not proceeded.

Superb public buildings occur at almoft every ftep through the Hague. At one end of the terrace, on which we were lodged, is the *Doelen*, a fpacious manfion, opening partly upon the *Tournois Veld*, or Place of Tournaments. The burgeffes here keep their colours, and, what is remarkable, ftill preferve the *infignia* of the *Toifon d'Or*, given to them by CHARLES the FIFTH.

Our WILLIAM the THIRD being admitted, at ten years of age, to the right of a burgefs here, was invefted with this order by the Burgomafter. At the other end of the terrace is the palace, built for Prince MAURICE of NASSAU, upon his return from the government of Brazil, by KAMPFEN, Lord of Rambroek, architect of the Stadthoufe at Amfterdam. The interior of this building was deftroyed by fire, in the commencement of the prefent century; but, the ftately walls of ftone and brick being uninjured, the rooms were reftored by the proprietors, affifted by a lottery. It is an inftance of the abundance of buildings here, that this palace is now chiefly ufed as a place of meeting, for the œconomical branch of the fociety of Haerlem, and for a fociety, inftituted here, for the encouragement of Dutch poetry.

The number of public buildings is much increafed by the houfes, which the eighteen towns provide for their Deputies, fent to the States

States of the Province. These are called the *Logements* of the several towns; and there has been a great deal of emulation, as to their magnificence. Amsterdam and Rotterdam have the finest.

The churches are not remarkable for antiquity, or grandeur. A congregation of English Protestants have their worship performed, in the manner of the Dissenters, in a small chapel near the *Vyver*, where we had the satisfaction to hear their venerable pastor, the Rev. Dr. M'CLEAN.

The residence of a Court at the Hague renders the appearance of the inhabitants less national and characteristic than elsewhere. There are few persons in the streets, who, without their orange cockades, might not be mistaken for English; but ribbons of this colour are almost universal, which some wear in their hats, and some upon a button-hole of the coat. The poorest persons, and there are more poor here than elsewhere,

elsewhere, find something orange-coloured to shew. Children have it placed upon their caps; so that the practice is carried to an extent as ridiculous, as the prohibition was in 1785, when the magistrates ordered, that *nothing orange-coloured should be worn, or shewn, not even fruits, or flowers, and that carrots should not be exposed to sale with the ends outwards.*

The distinctions between political classes are very strongly marked and preserved in Holland. We were informed, that there are some villages, in which the wearing of a cockade, and others, in which the want of one, would expose a passenger, especially a native, to insults. In the cities, where those of both parties must transact business together, the distinction is not much observed. In Amsterdam, the friends of the Stadtholder do not wear cockades. For the most part, the seamen, farmers and labouring classes in the towns are attached to the

Orange family, whose opponents are chiefly composed of the opulent merchants and tradesmen.

A history, or even a description of the two parties, if we were enabled to give it, would occupy too much space here; but it may be shortly mentioned, that the original, or chief cause of the dissension was, as might be expected, entirely of a commercial nature. The English interest had an unanimous popularity in Holland, about the year 1750. In the war of 1756, the French, having sustained a great loss of shipping, employed Dutch vessels to bring the produce of their American islands to Europe, and thus established a considerable connection with the merchants of Amsterdam and Rotterdam. The Court of Versailles took care, that the stream of French wealth, which they saw setting into the United Provinces, should carry with it some French politics; while the wealth itself effected more than all their contrivance,

contrivance, and gradually produced a kindnefs for France, efpecially in the province of Holland, through which it chiefly circulated. The Englifh Minifters took all Dutch fhips, having French property on board; and the popularity of England was for a time deftroyed. Several maritime towns, probably with fome inftigation from France, demanded a war againft England. The friends of the Stadtholder prevented this; and from that time the Prince began to fhare whatever unpopularity the meafures of the Englifh Minifters, or the induftry of the Englifh traders, could excite in a rival and a commercial country.

The capture of the French Weft India iflands foon after removed the caufe of the difpute; but the effects of it furvived in the jealoufy of the great cities towards the Stadtholder, and were much aggravated by the loffes of their merchants, at the commencement of hoftilities between England and the
United

United Provinces, in 1780. The Dutch fleet being then unprepared to fail, and every thing, which could float, having been sent out of the harbours of Yorkshire and Lincolnshire to intercept their trading ships, the fortunes of many of the most opulent houses in Holland were severely shook, and all their members became the enemies of the Stadtholder.

If to these circumstances it is added, that the province of Holland, which pays fifty-eight parts of every hundred, levied by taxes, has an ambition for acquiring greater influence in the general government, than is bestowed by its single vote, we have probably all the original causes of the party distinctions in Holland, though others may have been incorporated with others, during a long series of events and many violent struggles of the passions.

The Stadtholder, who has had the misfortune to attract so much attention by his difficulties,

difficulties, is said to be a man of plain manners and sound understanding, neither capable of political intrigue, nor inclined to it. His office requires, especially during a war, a great deal of substantial, personal labour, to which he devotes himself earnestly and continually, but which he has not the vigour to bear, without an evident oppression of spirits. We saw him at a parade of the Guards, and it is not necessary to be told of his labours to perceive how much he is affected by them. It is scarcely possible to conceive a countenance more expressive of a mind, always urged, always pressed upon, and not often receiving the relief of complete confidence in its efforts. His person is short and extremely corpulent; his air in conversation modest and mild. This attendance upon the parade is his chief exercise, or relaxation at the Hague, where he frequently passes ten of the hours between five in a morning and nine at night in his cabinet.

cabinet. He comes, accompanied by one or two officers, and his prefence produces no crowd. When we had viewed the parade and returned home, we faw him walking under our windows towards the *Voorhout*, accompanied by an officer, but not followed by a fingle perfon.

Converfation does not turn fo much upon the family of the Stadtholder, as that we could acquire any diftinct opinions of the other parts of it. Of his humanity and temper, there was fufficient proof, in 1787, when he returned to the Hague and was mafter of the perfons of thofe, who had lately banifhed him. Indeed, the conduct of both parties, with refpect to the perfonal fafety of their adverfaries, was honourable to the character of the nation. The States of Holland, during the prevalence of their authority, did not pretend, according to the injuftice of fimilar cafes, to any right of deftroying the friends of the Stadtholder,

who

who were in their hands; the Stadtholder, when he returned, and when the public deteſtation of his adverſaries was at an height, which would have permitted any meaſures againſt them, demanded no other retribution, than that ſeventeen, named in a liſt, ſhould be declared incapable of holding offices under the Republic.

One of the beſt excurſions from the Hague is made to the *Maiſon du Bois*, a ſmall palace of the Prince of ORANGE, in a wood, which commences almoſt at the northern gate of the town. This wood is called a park, but it is open to the public roads from Leyden, Haerlem and Amſterdam, which paſs through its noble alleys of oak and beech. It is remarkable for having ſo much attracted the regard of Philip the Second, that, in the campaign of 1574, he ordered his officers not to deſtroy it; and is probably the only thing, not deſtined for himſelf, of which this ample deſtroyer of human

human kind and of his own family ever directed the preservation. LOUIS the FOURTEENTH, probably having heard the praises of this care, left the mall of Utrecht to be a monument of similar tenderness, during an unprovoked invasion, which cost ten thousand lives.

The apartments of the *Maison du Bois* are very variously furnished. The best are fitted up with a light grey sattin, imbossed with Chinese birds and plants, in silk and feathers of the most beautiful tints; the window curtains, screens and coverings of the sophas and chairs are the same, and the frames of the latter are also of Chinese workmanship. Nothing more delicate and tasteful can be conceived; but, that you may not be quite distracted with admiration, the carpets are such as an English merchant would scarcely receive into a parlour. The furniture of the state bed-chamber is valuable, and has once been splendid; a light balustrade of curious
Japan

Japan work, about three feet high, runs across the room, and divides that part, in which the bed stands, from the remainder. The Princess's drawing-room, in which card parties are sometimes held, is well embellished with paintings, and may be called a superb apartment; but here again there is an instance of the incompleteness, said to be observable in the furniture of all rooms, out of England. Of four card tables two are odd ones, and literally would be despised in a broker's shop in London. The great glory of the house is the *Salle d'Orange*, an oblong saloon of noble height, with pannels, painted by nine celebrated painters of the Flemish and Dutch schools, among whom VAN TULDEN, a pupil of RUBENS, has observed his manner so much in a workshop of Vulcan and in a figure of Venus forming a trophy, that they have been usually attributed to his master. The subjects on the pannels and ceiling are all allegorical, and

compli-

complimentary, for the moſt part, to the Princes of the Houſe of Orange, eſpecially to FREDERIC HENRY, the ſon of the firſt WILLIAM and the grandſon of the Admiral COLIGNY. It was at the expence of his widow, that the houſe was built and the ſaloon thus ornamented.

Almoſt all the rooms are decorated with family portraits, of which ſome have juſt been contributed by the pencil of the Hereditary Princeſs. A large piece repreſents herſelf, taking a likeneſs of the Princeſs her mother-in-law, and includes what is ſaid to be an admirable portrait of her huſband. On the ſix doors of the grand cabinet are ſix whole lengths of ladies of the Houſe of Orange, exhibited in allegorical characters. The doors being covered by the paintings, when that, by which you have entered, is ſhut, you cannot tell the way back again. A portrait of LOUISA DE COLIGNY, the widow of William the Firſt, is enriched

with

with a painter's pun; she is presented by *Hope* with a branch of an *orange* tree, containing only *one* orange; from which the spectator is to learn, that her *son* was her *only hope*.

The most delightful outlet from the Hague is towards Schevening, a village on the sea-shore, nearly two miles distant, the road to which has been often and properly celebrated as a noble monument of tasteful grandeur. Commencing at the canal, which surrounds the Hague, it proceeds to the village through a vista so exactly straight, that the steeple of Schevening, the central object at the end of it, is visible at the first entrance. Four rows of lofty elms are planted along the road, of which the two central lines form this perfect and most picturesque vista; the others shelter paths on each side of it, for foot passengers.

The village itself, containing two or three hundred houses of fishermen and peasants,

G   would

would be a spectacle, for its neatness, any where but in Holland. There is no square, or street of the most magnificent houses in London, that can equal it for an universal appearance of freshness. It is positively bright with cleanliness; though its only street opens upon the sea, and is the resort of hundreds of fishermen. We passed a most delightful day at a little inn upon the beach, sometimes looking into the history of the village, which is very antient; then enquiring into its present condition; and then enjoying the prospect of the ocean, boundless to our view, on one side, and appearing to be but feebly restrained by a long tract of low white coast on the other.

The sea beats furiously upon the beach here, which has no doubt been much raised by art for the defence of the village. There is at least no other way of accounting for its security,[1] since 1574, between which year and the latter end of the preceding century,

it

HOLLAND.

it fuftained fix inundations. The firſt, in 1470, demoliſhed a church; the laſt waſhed away an hundred and twenty houſes; notwithſtanding which, the inhabitants built again upon their ſtormy ſhore; and their induſtry, that, at length, protected them from the ſea, enabled them to endure alſo the more inveterate ravages of the Spaniards. On this beach lie occaſionally great numbers of herring buſſes, too ſtoutly built to be injured by touching it. We ſuſpect our information to have been exaggerated; but we heard on the ſpot, that no leſs than one hundred and five belong to this village of little more than two hundred houſes, or are managed by agents in it. About forty were ſet on float by the tide in the afternoon, and, being hauled by means of anchors beyond a very heavy ſurf, were out of ſight, before we left the place.

It was amuſing to ſee the perſevering, effectual,

effectual, but not very active exertions of the seamen in this business, which could not often be more difficult than it then was, when a strong wind blew directly upon the shore. We here first perceived, what we had many other opportunities of observing, that, notwithstanding the general admiration of Dutch industry, it is of a nature which would scarcely acquire that name in England. A Dutchman of the labouring class is, indeed, seldom seen unemployed; but we never observed one man working hard, according to the English notion of the term. Perseverance, carefulness, and steadiness are theirs, beyond any rivalship; the vehemence, force, activity and impatience of an English sailor, or workman, are unknown to them. You will never see a Dutchman enduring the fatigue, or enjoying the rest, of a London porter. Heavy burthens, indeed, they do not carry. At Amsterdam, where carriages

riages are even fomewhat obnoxious, a cafk, holding four or five gallons of liquor, is removed by a horfe and a fledge.

On our way from Schevening, where a dinner cofts more than at an hotel in the Hague, we turned a little to the right to fee Portland Gardens, once the favourite refort of William and Mary; and faid to be laid out in the Englifh tafte. They are now a bad fpecimen even of Dutch gardens. The fituation is unufually low, having on one hand the raifed bank of the Schevening road, and, on another, the fand hills of the coaft. Between thefe, the moifture of the fea air is held for a long time, and finally drawn down upon the earth. The artificial ornaments are ftained and decaying; and the grafs and weeds of the neglected plots are capable only of a putrid green. Over walks of a black mould you are led to the orangery, where there is more decay, and may look through the windows of the green-houfe, houſe, to perceive how every thing is declining there. Some pavilions, provided with water ſpouts, are then to be ſeen; and, if you have the patience to wait the concluſion of an operation, intended to ſurpriſe you, you may count how many of the pipes refuſe to perform their office.

Nearer to the Hague, we were ſtopped to pay a toll of a few doights; a circumſtance which was attended with this proof of civility. Having paſſed in the morning, without the demand, we enquired why it ſhould be made now. The gatherer replied, that he had ſeen us paſs, but, knowing that we muſt return by the ſame way, had avoided giving more trouble than was neceſſary. This tax is paid for the ſupport of the bank, or digue, over which the road paſſes; a work, begun on the 1ſt of May 1664, and finiſhed on the 5th of December 1665, by the aſſiſtance of a loan granted for the enterpriſe. The breadth of the road is thirty-two yards.

The

The next day, after seeing the relief of the Stadtholder's *garde du corps*, the privates of which wear feathered hats, with uniforms of scarlet and gold, we left the Hague, with much admiration of its pleasantness and quiet grandeur, and took the *roof* of the trechtschuyt for Leyden.

LEYDEN.

THREE hours pleasant floating along a canal, adorned with frequent country houses, gardens, summer-houses and square balconies, or rather platforms, projecting over the water, within an hand's breadth of its level, brought us to this city, which was esteemed the second in Holland, before Rotterdam gained its present extent. Leyden is, however, so large, that a traveller is likely to have a walk of half a league to his inn; and those who arrive, as we did, at the time of the fair, may find the proceffion not very pleafant. We increafed our difficulties by turning away from he dirt and incivility of what was called the beft inn, and did not afterwards find a better, though fuch, it feems, might have been had.

Having, at length, become contented with the worft, we went towards the fair, of which we had as yet feen only the crowd. The booths, being difpofed under trees and along the borders of canals, made the whole appearance differ from that of an Englifh fair, though not quite fo much as we had expected. The ftock of the fhopkeepers makes a greater diftinction. There were feveral booths filled with filverfmiths' and jewellers' wares, to the amount of, probably, fome thoufand pounds each. Large French clocks in *or moulu* and porcelain were among their ftores. All the trades difplayed the moft valuable articles, that could be afked for in fimilar fhops in large cities.

We

We had the pleasure to see great quantities of English goods, and there were English names over three, or four of the booths.

The Dutch dresses were now become so familiar to us, that the crowd seemed as remarkable for the number of other persons in it, as for the abundance of peasants in their holiday finery, which, it is pleasant to know, displays the ornamental relics of several generations, fashion having very little influence in Holland. The fair occupied about a fourth part of the town, which we soon left to see the remainder. Two streets, parallel to each other, run through its whole length, and include the few public halls, of an University, which would scarcely be known to exist, if it had no more conspicuous objects than its buildings. The Dutch universities contain no endowed foundations; so that the professors, who have their salaries from the States, live in private houses, and the students in lodgings. The academical

mical drefs is worn only in the fchools, and by the profeffors. The library, to which Jofeph Scaliger was a benefactor, is open only once in a week, and then for no more than two hours. It is the conftant policy of the Dutch government, to make ftrangers leave as much money as poffible behind them; and Leyden was once fo greatly the refort of foreigners, that it was thought important not to let them read for nothing what they muft otherwife be obliged to buy.' The Univerfity is, of courfe, declining much, under this commercial wifdom of the magiftrates.

There are ftudents, however, of many nations and religions, no oaths being impofed, except upon the profeffors. Phyfic and botany efpecially are faid to be cultivated here with much fuccefs; and there is a garden, to which not only individuals, but the Eaft India Company, induftrioufly contribute foreign plants. The falaries of the
profeffors,

professors, who receive, besides, fees from the students, are nearly two hundred pounds a-year. The government of the University is in the Rector, who is chosen out of three persons returned by the Senate to the States; the Senate consists of the professors; and, on extraordinary occasions, the Senate and Rector are directed by Curators, who are the agents for the States.

The chief street in the town is of the crescent form, so that, with more public buildings, it would be a miniature resemblance of High-street, Oxford. The town-house is built with many spires, and with almost Chinese lightness. We did not see the interior of this, or, indeed, of any other public buildings; for, in the morning, when curiosity was to be indulged, our fastidiousness as to the inns returned, and induced us to take a passage for Haerlem. The MSS. of the Dutch version of the Bible, which are known to be deposited here, could not have
been

been shewn, being opened only once in three years, when the Deputies of the Synod and States attend; but we might have seen, in the town-house, some curious testimonies of the hardships and perseverance of the inhabitants, during the celebrated blockade of five months, in 1574, in confideration of which the University was founded.

After viewing some well-filled bookfellers' shops, and one wide street of magnificent houses, we again made half the circuit of this extensive city, in the way to the trecht-schuyt for

HAERLEM.

THE canal between Leyden and this place is nearly the pleasantest of the great number, which connect all the towns of the province with each other, and render them to the traveller a series of spectacles, almost

as

as easily visited as the amusements of one large metropolis. Though this is said to be one of the lowest parts of Holland, the country does not appear to have suffered more than the rest by water. The many country seats, which border the canals, are also proofs that it is thought to be well secured; yet this is the district, which has been proved, by indisputable observations, to be lower than the neighbouring sea, even in the profoundest calm. During the voyage, which was of four hours, we passed under several bridges, and saw numbers of smaller canals, crossing the country in various directions; but the passage of a trechtschuyt is not delayed for an instant by a bridge, the tow-rope being loosened from the boat, on one side, and immediately caught again, on the other, if it should not be delivered by some person, purposely stationed on the arch. It is not often that a canal makes any bend in its course; when

it

it does fo, there are fmall, high pofts at the point, round which the tow-rope is drawn; and, that the cord may not be deftroyed by the friction, the pofts fupport perpendicular rollers, which are turned by its motion. Such pofts and rollers might be advantageoufly brought into ufe in England. On moft of the canals are half-way villages, where paffengers may ftop, about five minutes, for refrefhment; but they will be left behind, without any ceremony, if they exceed the limited time, which the boatman employs in exchanging letters for fuch of the neighbouring country houfes as have not packet boxes placed on the banks.

Haerlem, like Leyden, is fortified by brick walls, but both feem to be without the folid earthen works, that conftitute the ftrength of modern fortreffes. A few pieces of cannon are planted near the gate, in order to command the bridge of a wide *foffé*; and the gate-houfe itfelf is a ftout building, deep enough

enough to render the paffage underneath fomewhat dark. There is otherwife very little appearance of the ftrength, that refifted the Duke of Alva, for twelve months, and exafperated his defire of vengeance fo far, that the murder of the inhabitants, who at laft furrendered to his promifes of protection, could alone appeafe it.

A narrow ftreet leads from the gate to the market-place, where two pieces of cannon are planted before the guard-houfe; the firft precaution againft internal commotion, which we had feen in the country. Haerlem had a great fhare in the difputes of 1787, and is faid to adhere more fully than any other city to the Anti-Stadtholderian politics of that period.

The market-place is very fpacious, and furrounds the great church, perhaps, the largeft facred building in the province of Holland. The lofty oak roof is marked with dates of the early part of the fixteenth century.

tury. The organ, sometimes said to be the best in Europe, is of unusual size, but has more power of sound than sweetness. The pipes are silvered, and the body carefully painted; for organs are the only objects in Dutch churches, which are permitted to be shewy. They are now building, in the great church at Rotterdam, a rival to this instrument, and need not despair of surpassing it.

A great part of the congregation sit upon chairs in the large aisle, which does not seem to be thought a much inferior place to the other parts. During an evening service, at which we were present, this was nearly filled; and while every person took a separate seat, women carried *chauffepieds*, or little wooden boxes, with pans of burning peat in them, to the ladies. This was on the 4th of June. The men enter the church with their hats on, and some wear them, during the whole service, with the most disgusting and arrogant hardihood.

We

We paffed a night at Haerlem, which is fcarcely worth fo long a ftay, though one ftreet, formed upon the banks of a canal, confifts of houfes more uniformly grand, than any out of the Hague, and furprifes you with its extenfive magnificence at a place, where there is little other appearance of wealth and none of fplendour. But the quietnefs of the Great in Holland is daily aftonifhing to a ftranger, who fometimes paffes through rows of palaces, without meeting a carriage, or a fervant. The inhabitants of thofe palaces have, however, not lefs earneft views, than they who are more agitated; the difference between them is, that the views of the former are only fuch as their fituation enables them to gratify, without the agitation of the latter. They can fit ftill and wait for the conclufion of every year, at which they are to be richer, or rather are to have much more money, than in the preceding one. They know,

that,

that, every day the silent progress of interest adds so much to their principal; and they are content to watch the course of time, for it is time alone that varies their wealth, the single object of their attention. There can be no motive, but its truth, for repeating the trite opinion of the influence of avarice in Holland: we expected, perhaps, with some vanity, to have found an opportunity for contradicting it; but are able only to add another testimony of its truth. The infatuation of loving money not as a means, but as an end, is paramount in the mind of almost every Dutchman, whatever may be his other dispositions and qualities; the addiction to it is fervent, inveterate, invincible, and universal from youth to the feeblest old age.

Haerlem has little trade, its communication with the sea being through Amsterdam, which latter place has always been able to

obstruct

obstruct the reasonable scheme of cutting a canal through the four miles of land, that separate the former from the ocean. Its manufactures of silk and thread are much less prosperous than formerly. Yet there are no symptoms of decay, or poverty, and the environs are well covered with gardens especially on the banks of the *Sparen*, of which one branch flows through the town and the other passes under the walls. Some charitable institutions, for the instruction and employment of children, should be mentioned also, to assuage the general censure of a too great fondness for money.

The house of LAURANCE COSTER, who is opposed to FAUST, GOTTENBURGH and SCHEFFER, for the honour of having invented the art of printing, is near the great church and is still inhabited by a bookseller. An inscription, not worth copying, asserts him to be the inventor. The house, which is small and stands in a row with others, must have received its present brick front in some time subsequent to that of COSTER.

AMSTERDAM.

THE voyage between Haerlem and this place is less pleasant, with respect to the country, than many of the other trips, but more gratifying to curiosity. For great part of the way, the canal passes between the lake, called *Haerlemer Maer*, and a large branch of the *Zuyder Zee*, called the River Y. In one place, the neck of land, which separates these two waters, is so thin, that a canal cannot be drawn through it; and, near this, there is a village, where passengers leave their first boat, another waiting for them at the renewal of the canal, within a quarter of a mile. Here, as upon other occasions of the same sort, nearly as much is

paid

paid for the carriage of two or three trunks between the boats, as for the whole voyage; and there is an *Ordonnatie* to authorize the price; for the Magiftrates have confidered, that thofe, who have much baggage, are probably foreigners, and may be thus made to fupport many of the natives. The Dutch themfelves put their linen into a velvet bag, called a *Ryfack*, and for this accordingly no charge is made.

The *Half Wegen Sluice* is the name of this feparation between two vaft waters, both of which have gained confiderably upon their fhores, and, if united, would be irrefiftible. At the narroweft part, it confifts pile-work and mafonry, to the thicknefs of probably forty feet. On this fpot the fpectator has, on his left hand, the Y, which, though called a river, is an immenfe inundation of the Zuyder Zee, and would probably carry a fmall veffel, without interruption, into the German ocean. On the other

other hand, is the Haerlem lake, about twelve miles long and nine broad, on which, during the fiege of Haerlem, the Dutch and Spaniards maintained fleets, and fought battles. Extending as far as Leyden, there is a paffage upon it from that city to Amfterdam, much fhorter than by the canal, but held to be dangerous. Before the year 1657, there was, however, no other way, and it was probably the lofs of the Prince of Bohemia and the danger of his dethroned father upon the lake, that inftigated the making of the canal.

This fluice is one of feveral valuable pofts, by which Amfterdam may be defended againft a powerful army, and was an important ftation, during the approach of the Duke of BRUNSWICK in 1787, when this city was the laft, which furrendered. All the roads being formed upon dikes, or embankments, may be defended by batteries; which can be attacked only by narrow columns

lumns and in front. The Half Wegen Sluice was, however, eafily taken by the Duke of BRUNSWICK, his opponents having neglected to place gun-boats on the Haerlem lake, over which he carried eight hundred men in thirty boats, and furprifed the Dutch before day-break, on the morning of the firft of October. This was one of his real affaults, but there were all together eleven made on that day, and, on the next, the city propofed to furrender.

Beyond the fluice, the canal paffes feveral breaches, made by inundations of the Y, and not capable of being drained, or repaired. In thefe places the canal is feparated from the inundations either by piles, or floating planks. None of the breaches were made within the memory of the prefent generation, yet the boatmen have learned to fpeak of them with horror.

There is nothing magnificent, or grand, in the approach to Amfterdam, or the prospect of the city. The sails of above an hundred windmills, moving on all sides, seem more conspicuous than the public buildings of this celebrated capital.

The trechtschuyt having stopped on the outside of the gate, we waited for one of the public coaches, which are always to be had by sending to a livery stable, but do not stand in the street for fares. It cost half-a-crown for a drive of about two miles into the city; the regulated price is a guilder, or twenty-pence. Our direction was to the *Doolen*; but the driver chose to take us to another inn, in the same street, which we did not discover to be otherwise called, till we had become satisfied with it.

Nearly all the chief thorough-fares of Amsterdam are narrow, but the carriages are neither so numerous as in other places of the same size, nor suffered to be driven with the same speed; so that, though there is no raised pavement, foot passengers are as safe

as

as elsewhere. There are broad terraces to the streets over the two chief canals, but these are sometimes encumbered by workshops, placed immediately over the water, between which and the houses the owners maintain an intercourse of packages and planks, with very little care about the freedom of the passage. This, indeed, may be constantly observed of the Dutch : they will never, either in their societies, or their business, employ their time, for a moment, in gratifying the little malice, or shewing the little envy, or assuming the little triumphs, which fill so much of life with unnecessary miseries ; but they will seldom step one inch out of their way, or surrender one moment of their time, to save those, whom they do not know, from any inconvenience. A Dutchman, throwing cheeses into his warehouse, or drawing iron along the pathway, will not stop, while a lady, or an infirm person passes, unless he perceives some-

somebody inclined to protect them; a warehouseman trundling a cask, or a woman in the favourite occupation of throwing water upon her windows, will leave it entirely to the passengers to take care of their limbs, or their clothes.

The canals themselves, which are the ornaments of other Dutch cities, are, for the most part, the nuisances of Amsterdam. Many of them are entirely stagnant; and, though deep, are so laden with filth, that, on a hot day, the feculence seems pestilential. Our windows opened upon two, but the scent very soon made us willing to relinquish the prospect. The bottoms are so muddy, that a boat-hook, drawn up, perhaps, through twelve feet of water, leaves a circle of slime at the top, which is not lost for many minutes. It is not unusual to see boats, laden with this mud, passing during mid-day, under the windows of the most opulent traders; and the fetid cargoes never disturb

disturb the intense studies of the counting-houses within.

After this distaste of the streets and canals of Amsterdam, it was a sort of duty to see, what is the glory of the city, the interior of the Stadthouse; but we lost this spectacle, by a negligence of that severe punctuality, in which the Dutch might be usefully imitated throughout the world. Our friends had obtained for us a ticket of admission at ten; we called upon them about half an hour afterwards; but, as the ride from their house would have required ten minutes more, the time of this ticket was thought to be elapsed. We would not accept one, which was offered to be obtained for another day, being unwilling to render it possible, that those, who were loading us with the sincerest civilities, should witness another apparent instance of inattention.

The Stadthouse, as to its exterior, is a plain stone building, attracting attention
chiefly

chiefly from its length, solidity and height. The front is an hundred and eight paces long. It has no large gate, but several small ones, and few statues, that would be observed, except one of Atlas on the top. The tales, as to the expence of the building, are inexhaustible. The foundation alone, which is entirely of piles, is said to have cost a million of guilders, or nearly ninety thousand pounds, and the whole edifice treble that sum. Its contents, the stock of the celebrated Bank, are estimated at various amounts, of which we will not repeat the lowest.

The Exchange is an humble building, and not convenient of access. The Post Office is well situated, upon a broad terrace, near the Stadthouse, and seems to be properly laid out for its use.

None of the churches are conspicuous for their structure; but the regulation, with respect to their ministers, should be more known.

HOLLAND.

known. Two are affigned to each, and all throughout the city have equal and refpectable falaries.

At a diftance from the Exchange are fome magnificent ftreets, raifed on the banks of canals, nearly equalling thofe of the Hague for the grandeur of houfes, and much exceeding in length the beft of Leyden and Haerlem. Thefe are the ftreets, which muft give a ftranger an opinion of the wealth of the city, while the Port, and that alone, can difplay the extenfivenefs of its commerce. The fhops and the preparations for traffic in the interior have a mean appearance to thofe, who try them by the ftandard of London conveniences and elegance.

The beft method of feeing the Port is to pafs down it in a boat to fome of the many towns, that fkirt the Zuyder Zee. One convenience, eafy to be had every where, is immediately vifible from the quays.

quays. Small platforms of planks supported by piles project from the shore between the vessels, which are disposed with their heads towards the sides of these little bridges; the furthest has thus a communication with the quay, and, if the cargo is not of very heavy articles, may be unladen at the same time with the others. The port is so wide, that, though both sides are thronged with shipping, the channel in the middle is, at least, as broad as the Thames at London Bridge; but the harbour does not extend to more than half the length of the *Pool* at London, and seems to contain about half the number of vessels. The form of the port is, however, much more advantageous for a display of shipping, which may be here seen nearly at one glance in a fine bay of the *Zuyder*.

After a sail of about an hour, we landed at Saardam, a village celebrated for the Dockyards, which supply Amsterdam with nearly

nearly all its fleets. A short channel carries vessels of the greatest burthen from Saardam to the Zuyder Zee, which the founders of the place took care not to approach too nearly; and the terrace at the end of this channel is prepared for the reception of cannon, that must easily defend it from any attack by sea. Though the neighbourhood of a dockyard might be supposed a sufficient antidote to cleanliness, the neatness of this little town renders it a spectacle even to the Dutch themselves. The streets are so carefully swept, that a piece of orange peel would be noticed upon the pavement, and the houses are washed and painted to the highest polish of nicety. Those, who are here in a morning, or at night, may probably see how many dirty operations are endured for the sake of this excessive cleanliness.

We were shewn nearly round the place, and, of course, to the cottage, in which the indefatigable

indefatigable Peter the First of Russia resided, when he was a workman in the dockyard. It is a tenement of two rooms, standing in a part of the village, so very mean, that the alleys near it are not cleaner, than those of other places. An old woman lives in the cottage, and subsists chiefly by shewing it to visitors, amongst whom have been the present Grand Duke and Duchess of Russia; for the Court of Petersburgh acknowledge it to have been the residence of Peter, and have struck a medal in commemoration of so truly honourable a palace. The old woman has received one of these medals from the present Empress, together with a grant of a small annuity to encourage her care of the cottage.

We passed an agreeable afternoon, at an inn on the terrace, from whence pleasure vessels and passage boats were continually departing for Amsterdam, and had a smart sail, on our return, during a cloudy and

somewhat

HOLLAND.

somewhat a stormy sunset. The approach to Amsterdam, on this side, is as grand as that from Haerlem is mean, half the circuit of the city, and all its spires, being visible at once over the crowded harbour. The great church of Haerlem is also seen at a small distance, on the right. The Amstel, a wide river, which flows through the city into the harbour, fills nearly all the canals, and is itself capable of receiving ships of considerable burthen: one of the bridges over it, and a terrace beyond, are among the few pleasant walks enjoyed by the inhabitants. The Admiralty, an immense building, in the interior of which is the dockyard, stands on this terrace, or quay; and the East India Company have their magazine here, instead of the interior of the city, where it would be benevolence to let its perfume counteract the noxiousness of the canals.

The government of Amsterdam is said to collect by taxes, rents and dues of various sorts, forts, more than an Englifh million and a half annually; and, though a great part of this fum is afterwards paid to the ufe of the whole Republic, the power of collecting and diftributing it muft give confiderable confequence to the magiftrates. The Senate, which has this power, confifts of thirty-fix members, who retain their feats during life, and were formerly chofen by the whole body of burghers; but, about two centuries ago, this privilege was furrendered to the Senate itfelf, who have ever fince filled up the vacancies in their number by a majority of their own voices. The *Echevins*, who form the court of juftice, are here chofen by the burghers out of a double number, nominated by the Senate: in the other cities, the Stadtholder, and not the burghers, makes this choice.

It is obvious, that when the City Senates, which return the Provincial States, and, through them, the States General, were
themfelves

HOLLAND.

themselves elected by the burghers, the legislature of the United Provinces had a character entirely representative; and, at present, a respect for public opinion is said to have considerable influence in directing the choice of the Senates.

The province of Holland, of which this city is the most important part, is supposed to contain 800,000 persons, who pay taxes to the amount of twenty-four millions of guilders, or two millions sterling, forming an average of two pounds ten shillings per person. In estimating the real taxation of a people, it is, however, necessary to consider the proportion of their consumption to their imports; for the duties, advanced upon imported articles, are not ultimately and finally paid till these are consumed. The frugal habits of the Dutch permit them to retain but a small part of the expensive commodities, which they collect; and the foreigners,

foreigners, to whom they are refold, pay, therefore, a large fhare of the taxation, which would be fo enormous, if it was confined to the inhabitants. Among the taxes, really paid by themfelves, are the following; —a land-tax of about four fhillings and nine pence per acre; a fale-tax of eight per cent. upon horfes, one and a quarter per cent. upon other moveables, and two and an half per cent. upon land and buildings; a tax upon inheritances out of the direct line, varying from two and an half to eleven per cent.; two per cent. upon every man's income; an excife of three pounds per hogfhead upon wine, and a charge of two per cent. upon all public offices. The latter tax is not quite fo popular here as in other countries, becaufe many of thefe offices are actually purchafed, the holders being compelled to buy ftock to a certain amount, and to deftroy the obligations. The excife upon on coffee, tea and salt is paid annually by each family, according to the number of their servants.

The inhabitants of Amsterdam, and some other cities, pay also a tax, in proportion to their property, for the maintenance of companies of city-guards, which are under the orders of their own magistrates. In Amsterdam, indeed, taxation is somewhat higher than in other places. Sir William Temple was assured, that no less than thirty duties might be reckoned to have been paid there, before a certain dish could be placed upon a table at a tavern.

The exact sums, paid by the several provinces towards every hundred thousand guilders, raised for the general use, have been often printed. The share of Holland is 58,309 guilders and a fraction; that of Overyssel, which is the smallest, 3571 guilders and a fraction.

Of five colleges of Admiralty, established within

within the United Provinces, three are in Holland, and contribute of courfe to point out the pre-eminence of that province. It is remarkable, that neither of thefe fupply their fhips with provifions: They allow the captains to deduct about four-pence halfpenny per day from the pay of each failor for that purpofe; a regulation, which is never made injurious to the feamen by any improper parfimony, and is fometimes ufeful to the public, in a country where preffing is not permitted. A captain, who has acquired a character for generofity amongft the failors, can mufter a crew in a few days, which, without fuch a temptation, could not be raifed in as many weeks.

We cannot fpeak with exactnefs of the prices of provifions in this province, but they are generally faid to be as high as in England. The charges at inns are the fame as on the roads within an hundred miles of London, or, perhaps, fomething more. Port wine

wine is not so common as a wine which they call Claret, but which is compounded of a strong red wine from Valencia, mixed with some from Bourdeaux. The general price for this is twenty pence English a bottle; three and four pence is the price for a much better sort. About half-a-crown per day is charged for each apartment; and *logement* is always the first article in a bill.

Private families buy good claret at the rate of about eighteen pence per bottle, and chocolate for two shillings per pound. Beef is sold for much less than in England, but is so poor that the Dutch use it chiefly for soup, and salt even that which they roast. Good white sugar is eighteen pence per pound. Bread is dearer than in England; and there is a sort, called milk bread, of uncommon whiteness, which costs nearly twice as much as our ordinary loaves. Herbs and fruits are much lower priced, and worfe in flavour; but their colour and fize are not inferior. Fifh is cheaper than in our maritime counties, thofe excepted which are at a great diftance from the metropolis. Coffee is very cheap, and is more ufed than tea. No kind of meat is fo good as in England; but veal is not much inferior, and is often dreffed as plainly and as well as with us. The innkeepers have a notion of mutton and lamb chops; but then it is *à la Maintenon*; and the rank oil of the paper is not a very delightful fauce. Butter is ufually brought to table *clarified*, that is, purpofely melted into an *oil*; and it is difficult to make them underftand that it may be otherwife.

The Dutch have much more refpect for Englifh than for other travellers; but there is a jealoufy, with refpect to our commerce, which is avowed by thofe, who have been tutored to calm difcuffion, and may be perceived in the converfation of others,

whenever

whenever the state of the two countries is noticed. This jealousy is greater in the maritime than in the other provinces, and in Amsterdam than in some of the other cities: Rotterdam has so much direct intercourse with England, as to feel, in some degree, a share in its interests.

Some of our excursions round Amsterdam were made in a curious vehicle; the body of a coach placed upon a sledge, and drawn by one horse. The driver walks by the side, with the reins in one hand, and in the other a wetted rope, which he sometimes throws under the sledge to prevent it from taking fire, and to fill up the little gaps in the pavement. The appearance of these things was so whimsical, that curiosity tempted us to embark in one; and, finding them laughed at by none but ourselves, the convenience of being upon a level with the shops, and with the faces that seemed to contain the history of the shops, induced us

to

to use them again. There are great numbers of them, being encouraged by the magistrates, in preference to wheel carriages, and, as is said, in tenderness to the piled foundations of the city, the only one in Holland in which they are used. The price is eight pence for any distance within the city, and eight pence an hour for attendance.

Near Amsterdam is the small village of Ouderkirk, a place of some importance in the short campaign of 1787, being accessible by four roads, all of which were then fortified. It consists chiefly of the country houses of Amsterdam merchants, at one of which we passed a pleasant day. Having been but slightly defended, after the loss of the posts of *Half Wegen* and *Amstelreen*, it was not much injured by the Prussians; but there are many traces of balls thrown into it. The ride to it from Amsterdam is upon the chearful banks of the Amstel, which is bordered,

bordered, for more than five miles, with gardens of better verdure and richer groves than had hitherto appeared. The village was fpread with booths for a fair, though it was Sunday; and we were fomewhat furprifed to obferve, that a people in general fo gravely decorous as the Dutch, fhould not pay a ftricter deference to the Sabbath. We here took leave of fome friends, whofe frank manners and obliging difpofitions are remembered with much more delight than any other circumftances, relative to Amfterdam.

UTRECHT.

The paffage from Amfterdam hither is of eight hours; and, notwithftanding the pleafantnefs of trechtfchuyt conveyance, feemed fomewhat tedious, after the habit of paffing from city to city in half that time.
The

The canal is, however, juftly preferred to others, on account of the richnefs of its furrounding fcenery; and it is pleafing to obferve how gradually the country improves, as the diftance from the province of Holland and from the fea increafes. Towards Utrecht, the gardens rife from the banks of the canal, inftead of fpreading below its level, and the grounds maintain avenues and plantations of lofty trees. Vegetation is ftronger and more copious; fhrubs rife to a greater height; meadows difplay a livelier green; and the lattice-work of the bowery avenues, which occur fo frequently, ceafes to be more confpicuous than the foliage.

It was Whitfuntide, and the banks of the canal were gay with holiday people, riding in waggons and carts; the latter frequently carrying a woman wearing a painted hat as large as an umbrella, and a man with one in whimfical contraft clipped nearly clofe to the crown. The lady fometimes

times refreshed herself with a fan, and the gentleman, meanwhile, with a pipe of tobacco. Every village we passed resounded with hoarse music and the clatter of wooden shoes: among these the prettiest was *Nieuverfluys*, bordering each side of the canal, with a white drawbridge picturesquely shadowed with high trees, and green banks sloping to the water's brim. Pleasure-boats and trechtschuyts lined the shores; and the windows of every house were thronged with broad faces. On the little terraces below were groups of smokers, and of girls in the neat trim Dutch dress, with the fair complexion and air of decorous modesty, by which their country-women are distinguished.

About half way from Amsterdam stands a small modern fortification; and it is an instance of Dutch carefulness, that grass had just been mowed even from the parapets of the batteries, and was made up in heaps

within

within the works. Not far from it is an ancient castle of one tower, left in the state to which it was reduced during the contest with the Spaniards.

Near Utrecht, the ground has improved so much, that nothing but its evenness distinguishes it from other countries; and, at some distance eastward, the hills of Guelderland rise to destroy this last difference. The entrance into the city is between high terraces, from which steps descend to the canal; but the street is not wide enough to have its appearance improved by this sort of approach. Warehouses, formed under the terraces, shew also that the latter have been raised more for convenience than splendour.

The steeple of the great church, formerly a cathedral, excites, in the mean time, an expectation of dignity in the interior, where some considerable streets and another canal complete the air of an opulent city. It is

not

not immediately feen, that a great part of the body of this cathedral has been deftroyed, and that the canals, being fubject to tides, have dirty walls during the ebb. The fplendour, which might be expected in the capital of a province much inhabited by nobility, does not appear; nor is there, perhaps, any ftreet equal to the beft of Leyden and Haerlem; yet, in general beauty, the city is fuperior to either of thefe.

We arrived juft before nine, at which hour a bell rings to denote the fhutting of the larger gates; for the rules of a walled town are obferved here, though the fortifications could be of little other ufe than to prevent a furprife by horfe. The *Chateau d'Anvers*, at which we lodged, is an excellent inn, with a landlord, who tells, that he has walked fixty years in his own paffage, and that he had the honour of entertaining the Marquis of Granby thirteen times, during the war of 1756. Though the Dutch

inns

inns are generally unobjectionable, there is an air of English completeness about this which the others do not reach.

Utrecht is an university, but with as little appearance of such an institution as Leyden. The students have no academical dress; and their halls, which are used only for lectures and exercises, are formed in the cloisters of the ancient cathedral. The chief sign of their residence in the place is, that the householders, who have lodgings to let, write upon a board, as is done at Leyden, *Cubicula locanda.* We were shewn round the town by a member of the university, who carefully avoided the halls; and we did not press to see them.

There are still some traces remaining of the Bishopric, which was once so powerful, as to excite the jealousy, or rather, perhaps, to tempt the avarice of Charles the Fifth, who seized upon many of its possessions. The use made of the remainder by the

States

States General, is scarcely more justifiable; for the prebends still subsist, and are disposed of by sale to Lay Canons, who send delegates to the Provincial States, as if they had ecclesiastical characters.

The substantial remains of the Cathedral are one aisle, in which divine service is performed, and a lofty, magnificent Gothic tower, that stands apart from it. The ascent of this tower is one of the tasks prescribed to strangers, and, laborious as it is, the view from the summit sufficiently rewards them. A stone staircase, steep, narrow, and winding, after passing several grated doors, leads into a floor, which you hope is at the top, but which is little more than half way up. Here the family of the belfryman fill several decently furnished apartments, and shew the great bell, with several others, the noise of which, it might be supposed, no human ears could bear, as they must, at the distance of only three, or four yards. After resting a

K   few

few minutes in a room, the windows of which command, perhaps, a more extensive land view than any other inhabited apartment in Europe, you begin the second ascent by a staircase still narrower and steeper, and, when you seem to be so weary as to be incapable of another step, half the horizon suddenly bursts upon the view, and all your meditated complaints are overborne by expressions of admiration.

Towards the west, the prospect, after including the rich plain of gardens near Utrecht, extends over the province of Holland, intersected with water, speckled with towns, and finally bounded by the sea, the mists of which hide the low shores from the sight. To the northward, the Zuyder Zee spreads its haziness over Amsterdam and Naerden; but from thence to the east, the spires of Amersfoort, Rhenen, Arnheim, Nimeguen and many intermediate towns, are seen amongst the woods and hills, that

gradually

gradually rife towards Germany. Southward, the more mountainous diftrict of Cleves and then the level parts of Guelderland and Holland, with the windings of the Waal and the Leck, in which the Rhine lofes itfelf, complete a circle of probably more than fixty miles diameter, that ftrains the fight from this tremendous fteeple. The almoft perpendicular view into the ftreets of Utrecht affords afterwards fome relief to the eye, but increafes any notions of danger, you may have had from obferving, that the open work Gothic parapet, which alone prevents you from falling with dizzinefs, has fuffered fomething in the general decay of the church.

While we were at the top, the bells ftruck; and, between the giddinefs communicated by the eye, and the ftunning effect of a found that feemed to fhake the fteeple, we were compelled to conclude fooner than had been intended this comprehensive and farewell prospect of Holland.

The Mall, which is esteemed the chief ornament of Utrecht, is, perhaps, the only avenue of the sort in Europe, still fit to be used for the game that gives its name to them all. The several rows of noble trees include, at the sides, roads and walks; but the centre is laid out for the game of *Mall*, and, though not often used, is in perfect preservation. It is divided so as to admit of two parties of players at once, and the side-boards sufficiently restrain spectators. The Mall in St. James's Park was kept in the same state, till 1752, when the present great walk was formed over the part, which was separated by similar side-boards. The length of that at Utrecht is nearly three quarters of a mile. The luxuriance and loftiness of the trees preserve a perspective much superior to that of St. James's, but in the

HOLLAND.

the latter the whole breadth of; the walks is greater, and the view is more extenfive, as well as more ornamented.

This city, being a fort of capital to the neighbouring nobility, is called the politeft in the United Provinces, and certainly abounds, more than the others, with the profeffions and trades, which are fubfervient to fplendour. One practice, obferved in fome degree, in all the cities, is moft frequent here; that of bows paid to all parties, in which there are ladies, by every gentleman who paffes. There are, however, no plays, or other public amufements; and the feftivities, or ceremonies, by which other nations commemorate the happier events in their hiftory, are as unufual here as in the other parts of the United Provinces, where there are more occafions to celebrate and fewer celebrations than in moft European countries. Mufic is very little cultivated in any of the cities, and plays are to be feen only at Amſterdam and the Hague, where German and Dutch pieces are acted upon alternate nights. At Amſterdam, a French Opera-houſe has been ſhut up, and, at the Hague, a *Comédie*, and the actors ordered to leave the country.

The ramparts of the city, which are high and command extenſive proſpects, are rather emblems of the peacefulneſs, which it has long enjoyed, than ſigns of any effectual reſiſtance, prepared for an enemy. They are in many places regularly planted with trees, which muſt be old enough to have been ſpared, together with the Mall, by Louis the Fourteenth; in others, pleaſure houſes, inſtead of batteries, have been raiſed upon them. A few pieces of old cannon are planted for the purpoſe of ſaluting the Prince of ORANGE, when he paſſes the city.

Trechtſchuyts go no further eaſtward than this place, ſo that we hired a voiturier's rier's carriage, a fort of curricle with a driver's box in front, for the journey to Nimeguen. The price for thirty-eight, or thirty-nine miles, was fomething more than a guinea and a half; the horfes were worth probably fixty pounds upon the fpot, and were as able as they were fhowy, or they could not have drawn us through the deep fands, that cover one third of the road.

We were now fpeedily quitting almoft every thing, that is generally characteriftic of Dutch land. The paftures were intermixed with fields of profperous corn; the beft houfes were furrounded by high woods, and the grounds were feparated by hedges, inftead of water, where any fort of partition was ufed. Windmills were feldom feen, and thofe only for corn. But thefe improvements in the appearance of the country were accompanied by many fymptoms of a diminifhed profperity among the people. In eight-and-thirty miles there was not one confiderable

confiderable town; a fpace, which, in the province of Holland, would probably have included three opulent cities, feveral extenfive villages, and ranges of manfions, erected by merchants and manufacturers.

Wyk de Duerſtede, the firſt town in the road, is diſtinguiſhable at ſome diſtance, by the ſhattered tower of its church, a monument of the defolation, fpread by the Spaniards. The inhabitants, probably intending, that it ſhould remain as a leſſon to poſterity, have not attempted to reſtore it, further than to place ſome ſtones over the part filled by the clock. The body of the church and the remainder of the tower are not deficient of Gothic dignity. The town itſelf conſiſts of one, or two wide ſtreets, not well filled either with inhabitants, or houſes.

The road here turns to the eaſtward and is led along the right bank of the Leck, one of the branches of the Rhine, upon a

raiſed

raifed mound, or dique, fometimes twenty, or thirty feet, above the river on the one fide, and the plains, on the other. Small pofts, each numbered, are placed along this road, at unequal diftances, for no other ufe, which we could difcover, than to enable the furveyors to report exactly where the mound may want repairs. The carriage way is formed of a deep fand, which we were very glad to leave, by croffing the river at a ferry; though this road had given us a fine view of its courfe and of fome ftately veffels, preffing againft the ftream, on their voyage to Germany.

On the other fide, the road went further from the river, though we continued to fkirt it occafionally as far as a fmall ferry-houfe, oppofite to Rhenen, at which we dined, while the horfes refted under a fhed, built over the road, as weigh-houfes are at our turnpikes. Rhenen is a walled town, built

upon

upon an ascent from the water, and appears to have two, or three neat streets.

Having dined in a room, where a table, large enough for twenty persons, was placed, on one side, and a line of four, or five beds, covered by one long curtain, was formed against the wainscot, on the other, the voiturier clamoured, that the gates of Nimeguen would be shut before we could get to them, and we soon began to cross the country between the Leck and the Waal, another branch of the Rhine, which, in Guelderland, divides itself into so many channels, that none can be allowed the pre-eminence of retaining its name. Soon after reaching the right bank of the Waal, the road affords a view of the distant towers of Nimeguen, which appear there to be very important, standing upon a brow, that seems to front the whole stream of the river. In the way, we passed several noble estates, with man-

sions,

HOLLAND.

fions, built in the caftellated form, which James the Firft introduced into England, inftead of the more fortified refidences; and there was a fufficient grandeur of woods and avenues, to fhew, that there might be parks, if the owners had the tafte to form them. Between the avenues, the gilded ornaments of the roof, and the peaked coverings, placed, in fummer, over the chimneys, glittered to the light, and fhewed the fantaftic ftyle of the architecture, fo exactly copied in Flemifh landfcapes of the fixteenth and feventeenth centuries.

As the fun declined and we drew near Nimeguen, the various colouring of a fcene more rich than extenfive rendered its effect highly interefting. The wide Waal on our left, reflecting the evening blufh, and a veffel whofe full fails caught a yellow gleam from the weft; the ramparts and pointed roofs of Nimeguen rifing over each other, juft tinted by the vapour that afcended from

the

the bay below; the faint and fainter blue of two ridges of hills in Germany retiring in the distance, with the mellow green of nearer woods and meadows, formed a combination of hues surprisingly gay and beautiful. But Nimeguen lost much of its dignity on a nearer approach; for many of the towers, which the treachery of fancy had painted at distance, changed into forms less picturesque; and its situation, which a bold sweep of the Waal had represented to be on a rising peninsula crowning the flood, was found to be only on a steep beside it. The ramparts, however, the high old tower of the citadel, the Belvidere, with the southern gate of the town beneath, composed part of an interesting picture on the opposite margin of the river. But there was very little time to observe it: the driver saw the flying bridge, making its last voyage, for the night, towards our shore, and likely to return in about twenty minutes; he, therefore,

therefore, drove furiously along the high bank of the river, and, turning the angle of the two roads with a velocity, which would have done honour to a Brentford postillion, entered that adjoining the first half of the bridge, and shewed the directors of the other half, that we were to be part of their cargo.

This bridge, which is partly laid over boats and partly over two barges, that float from the boats to the shore, is so divided, because the stream is occasionally too rapid to permit an entire range of boats between the two banks. It is thus, for one half, a bridge of boats, and, for the other, a flying bridge; which last part is capable of containing several carriages, and joins to the other so exactly as not to occasion the least interruption. It is also railed for the safety of foot passengers, of whom there are commonly twenty, or thirty. The price for a carriage is something about twenty-pence,
which

which the tollmen carefully collect as soon as the demi-bridge has begun its voyage.

NIMEGUEN

Has, towards the water, little other fortification than an antient brick wall, and a gate. Though it is a garrison town, and certainly no trifling object, we were not detained at the gate by troublesome ceremonies. The commander, affecting no unnecessary carefulness, is satisfied with a copy of the report, which the innkeepers, in all the towns, send to the Magistrates, of the names and conditions of their guests. A printed paper is usually brought up, after supper, in which you are asked to write your name, addition, residence, how long you intend to stay, and to whom you are known in the province. We did not shew a passport in Holland.

The

The town has an abrupt but short elevation from the river, which you ascend by a narrow but clean street, opening into a spacious market-place. The great church and the guard-house are on one side of this; from the other, a street runs to the eastern gate of the town, formed in the old wall, beyond which commence the modern and strong fortifications, that defend it, on the land side. At the eastern extremity of the place, a small mall leads to the house, in which the Prince of Orange resided, during the troubles of 1786; and, beyond it, on a sudden promontory towards the river, stands a prospect house, called the Belvidere, which, from its eastern and southern windows, commands a long view into Germany, and to the north looks over Guelderland. From this place all the fortifications, which are very extensive, are plainly seen, and a military person might estimate their strength. There are several forts and outworks,

works, and, though the ditch is pallifadoed inftead of filled, the place muft be capable of a confiderable defence, unlefs the befieging army fhould be mafters of the river and the oppofite bank. There was formerly a fortrefs upon this bank, which was often won and loft, during the fieges of Nimeguen, but no remains of it are vifible now.

The town is claffic ground to thofe, who venerate the efforts, by which the provinces were refcued from the dominion of the Spaniards. It was firft attempted by SENGIUS, a Commander in the Earl of LEICESTER's army, who propofed to enter it, at night, from the river, through a houfe, which was to be opened to him; but his troops by miftake entered another, where a large company was collected, on occafion of a wedding, and, being thus difcovered to the garrifon, great numbers of thofe, already landed upon the beach, were put to the fword, or drowned in the confufion of

the

the retreat. An attempt by Prince Maurice to furprife it was defeated by the failure of a *petard*, applied to one of the gates; but it was foon after taken by a regular fiege, carried on chiefly from the other fide of the river. This and the neighbouring fortrefs of Grave were among the places, firft taken by Louis the Fourteenth, during his invafion, having been left without fufficient garrifons.

The citadel, a remnant of the antient fortifications, is near the eaftern gate, which appears to be thought ftronger than the others, for, on this fide, alfo is the arfenal.

Nimeguen has been compared to Nottingham, which it refembles more in fituation than in ftructure, though many of the ftreets are fteep, and the windows of one range of houfes fometimes overlook the chimnies of another; the views alfo, as from fome parts of Nottingham, are over a green and extenfive level, rifing into diftant hills;

and here the comparison ends. The houses are built entirely in the Dutch fashion, with many coloured, painted fronts, terminating in peaked roofs; but some decline of neatness may be observed by those who arrive here from the province of Holland. The market-place, though gay and large, cannot be compared with that of Nottingham, in extent, nor is the town more than half the size of the latter, though it is said to contain nearly fifty thousand inhabitants. From almost every part of it you have, however, a glimpse of the surrounding landscape, which is more extensive than that seen from Nottingham, and is adorned by the sweeps of a river of much greater dignity than the Trent.

We left Nimeguen, in the afternoon, with a voiturier, whose price, according to the *ordonnatie*, was higher than if we had set out half an hour sooner, upon the supposition that he could not return that night.

night. The road lies through part of the fortifications, concerning which there can, of courfe, be no fecrecy. It then enters an extenfive plain, and runs almoft parallel to a range of heights, at the extremity of which Nimeguen ftands, and prefents an appearance of ftill greater ftrength and importance than when feen from the weftward.

After a few miles, this road leaves the territories of the United Provinces, and enters the Pruffian duchy of Cleves, at a fpot where a mill is in one country, and the miller's houfe in the other. An inftance of difference between the conditions of the people in the two countries was obfervable even at this paffage of their boundary. Our poftillion bought, at the miller's, a loaf of black bread, fuch as is not made

made in the Dutch provinces, and carried it away for the food of his horses, which were thus initiated into some of the blessings of the German peasantry. After another quarter of a mile you have more proofs that you have entered the country of the King of Prussia. From almost every cluster of huts barefooted children run out to beg, and ten or a dozen stand at every gate, nearly throwing themselves under the wheels to catch your money, which, every now and then, the bigger seize from the less.

Yet the land is not ill-cultivated. The distinction between the culture of land in free and arbitrary countries, was, indeed, never very apparent to us, who should have been ready enough to perceive it. The great landholders know what should be done, and the peasantry are directed to do it. The latter are, perhaps, supplied with stock, and the grounds produce as much as elsewhere,

elsewhere, though you may read, in the looks and manners of the people, that very little of its productions is for them.

Approaching nearer to Cleves, we travelled on a ridge of heights, and were once more cheared with the "pomp of groves." Between the branches were delightful catches of extensive landscapes, varied with hills clothed to their summits with wood, where frequently the distant spires of a town peeped out most picturesquely. The open vales between were chiefly spread with corn; and such a prospect of undulating ground, and of hills tufted with the grandeur of forests, was inexpressibly chearing to eyes fatigued by the long view of level countries.

At a few miles from Cleves the road enters the Park and a close avenue of noble plane-trees, when these prospects are, for a while, excluded. The first opening is where, on one hand, a second avenue commences, and, on the other, a sort of broad bay in the woods, which were planted by Prince Maurice, includes an handfome houfe now converted into an inn, which, owing to the pleafantnefs of the fituation, and its vicinity to a mineral fpring, is much frequented in fummer. A ftatue of General Martin Schenck, of dark bronze, in complete armour, and with the beaver down, is raifed upon a lofty Ionic column, in the centre of the avenue, before the houfe. Refting upon a lance, the figure feems to look down upon the paffenger, and to watch over the fcene, with the fternnefs of an ancient knight. It appears to be formed with remarkable fkill, and has an air more ftriking and grand than can be readily defcribed.

The *orangerie* of the palace is ftill preferved, together with a femi-circular pavilion, in a recefs of the woods, through which an avenue of two miles leads you to

CLEVES.

CLEVES.

This place, which, being the capital of a duchy, is entitled a City, confifts of fome irregular ftreets, built upon the brow of a fteep hill. It is walled, but cannot be mentioned as fortified, having no folid works. The houfes are chiefly built of ftone, and there is a little of Dutch cleanlinefs; but the marks of decay are ftrongly impreffed upon them, and on the ancient walls. What little trade there is, exifts in retailing goods fent from Holland. The Dutch language and coins are in circulation here, almoft as much as the German.

The eftablifhed religion of the town is Proteftant; but here is an almoft univerfal toleration, and the Catholics have feveral churches and monafteries. Cleves has fuffered a various fate in the fport of war during

during many centuries, but has now little to diftinguifh it except the beauty of its profpects, which extend into Guelderland and the province of Holland, over a country enriched with woody hills and vallies of corn and pafturage.

Being convinced, in two or three hours, that there was nothing to require a longer ftay, we fet out for Xanten, a town in the fame duchy, diftant about eighteen miles. For nearly the whole of this length the road lay through a broad avenue, which frequently entered a foreft of oak, fir, elm, and majeftic plane-trees, and emerged from it only to wind along its fkirts. The views then opened over a country, diverfified with gentle hills, and ornamented by number-lefs fpires upon the heights, every fmall town having feveral convents. The caftle of Eltenberg, on the fummit of a wooded mountain, was vifible during the whole of this ftage and part of the next day's journey.

ney. Yet the fewnefs, or the poverty, of the inhabitants appeared from our meeting only one chaife, and two or three fmall carts, for eighteen miles of the only high-road in the country.

It was a fine evening in June, and the rich lights, thrown among the foreft glades, with the folitary calmnefs of the fcene, and the ferenenefs of the air, filled with fcents from the woods, were circumftances which perfuaded to fuch tranquil rapture as Collins muft have felt when he had the happinefs to addrefs to Evening—

> For when thy folding ftar, arifing, fhews
> His paly circlet, at his warning lamp,
> The fragrant hours and elves
> Who flept in buds the day:
>
> And many a nymph, who wreaths her
>   brows with fedge,
> And fheds the frefh'ning dew, and, lovelier ftill,

The

The pensive pleasures sweet
Prepare thy shadowy car.

A small half-way village, a stately convent, with its gardens, called Marienbaum, founded in the 15th century by Maria, Duchess of Cleves, and a few mud cottages of the woodcutters, were the only buildings on the road: the foot passengers were two Prussian soldiers. It was moonlight, and we became impatient to reach Xanten, long before our driver could say, in a mixture of German and Dutch, that we were near it. At length from the woods, that had concealed the town, a few lights appeared over the walls, and dissipated some gloomy fancies about a night to be passed in a forest.

XANTEN.

XANTEN.

THIS is a small town, near the Rhine, without much appearance of prosperity, but neater than most of the others around it. Several narrow streets open into a wide and pleasant market-place, in the centre of which an old but flourishing elm has its branches carefully extended by a circular railing, to form an arbour over benches. A cathedral, that proves the town to have been once more considerable, is on the north side of this place; a fine building, which, shewn by the moon of a summer midnight, when only the bell of the adjoining convent calling the monks to prayers, and the waving of the aged tree, were to be heard, presented a scene before the windows of our inn, that fully recompensed for its want of accommodation.

There were also humbler reasons towards contentment; for the people of the house were extremely desirous to afford it; and the landlord was an orator in French, of which and his address he was pleasantly vain. He received us with an air of humour, mingled with his complaisance, and hoped, that, " as *Monsieur* was *Anglois*, he should surprise him with his *vin extraordinaire*, all the Rhenish wine being adulterated by the Dutch, before they sent it to England. His house could not be fine, because he had little money; but he had an excellent cook, otherwise it could not be expected that the prebendaries of the cathedral would dine at it, every day, and become, as they were, *vraiment, Monsieur, gros comme vous me voyez!*"

There are in this small town several monasteries and one convent of noble canonesses, of which last the members are few, and the revenues very great. The interior
of

of the cathedral is nearly as grand as the outside; and mass is performed in it with more solemnity than in many, which have larger institutions.

We left Xanten, the next morning, in high spirits, expecting to reach Cologne, which was little more than fifty miles distant, before night, though the landlord and the postmaster hinted, that we should go no further than Neuss. This was our first use of the German post, the slowness of which, though it has been so often described, we had not estimated. The day was intensely hot, and the road, unsheltered by trees, lay over deep sands, that reflected the rays. The refreshing forests of yesterday we now severely regretted, and watched impatiently to catch a freer air from the summit of every hill on the way. The postillion would permit his horses to do little more than walk, and every step threw up heaps of dust into the chaise. It had been so often

said

said by travellers, that money has as little effect in such cases as intreaties, or threats, that we supposed this slowness irremediable, which was really intended only to produce an offer of what we would willingly have given.

RHEINBERG.

IN something more than three hours, we reached Rheinberg, distant about nine miles; a place often mentioned in the military history of the sixteenth and seventeenth centuries, and which we had supposed would at least gratify us by the shew of magnificent ruins, together with some remains of its former importance. It is a wretched place of one dirty street, and three or four hundred mean houses, surrounded by a decayed wall that never was grand, and half filled by inhabitants, whose indolence, while

it

it is probably more to be pitied than blamed, accounts for the fullenneſs and wretchedneſs of their appearance. Not one ſymptom of labour, or comfort, was to be perceived in the whole town. The men ſeemed, for the moſt part, to be ſtanding at their doors, in unbuckled ſhoes and woollen caps. What few women we ſaw were brown, without the appearance of health, which their leanneſs and dirtineſs prevented. Some ſmall ſhops of huckſters' wares were the only ſigns of trade.

The inn, that ſeemed to be the beſt, was ſuch as might be expected in a remote village, in a croſs road in England. The landlord was ſtanding before the door in his cap, and remained there ſome time after we had found the way into a ſitting room, and from thence, for want of attendance, into a kitchen; where two women, without ſtockings, were watching over ſome ſort of cookery in earthen jugs. We were ſupplied,

at

at length, with bread, butter and four wine, and did not fuffer ourfelves to confider this as any fpecimen of German towns, becaufe Rheinberg was not a ftation of the poft; a delufion, the fpirit of which continued through feveral weeks, for we were always finding reafons to believe, that the wretchednefs of prefent places and perfons was produced by fome circumftances, which would not operate in other diftricts.

This is the condition of a town, which, in the fixteenth and feventeenth centuries, was thought important enough to be five times attacked by large armies. FARNESE, the Spanifh commander, was diverted from his attempt upon it, by the neceffity of relieving Zutphen, then befieged by the Earl of Leicefter: in 1589, the Marquis of Varambon invefted it, for the Spaniards, by order of the Prince of Parma; but it was relieved by our Colonel Vere, who, after a long battle, completely defeated the Spanifh army.

army. In 1599, when it was attacked by Mendoza, a magazine caught fire. The governor, his family, and a part of the garrifon were buried in the ruins of a tower, and the explofion funk feveral veffels in the Rhine; after which, the remainder of the garrifon furrendered the place. The Prince of Orange retook it in 1633. Four years afterwards, the Spaniards attempted to furprife it in the night; but the Deputy Governor and others, who perceived that the garrifon could not be immediately collected, paffed the walls, and, pretending to be deferters, mingled with the enemy, whom they perfuaded to delay the attack for a few minutes. The troops within were in the mean time prepared for their defence, and fucceeded in it; but the Governor, with two officers and fifteen foldiers who had accompanied him, being difcovered, were killed. All thefe contefts were for a place not belonging to either party, being in the

electorate

electorate of Cologne, but which was valuable to both, for its neighbourhood to their frontiers.

Beyond Rheinberg, our prospects were extensive, but not so woody, or so rich as those of the day before, and few villages enlivened the landscape. Open corn lands, intermixed with fields of turnips, spread to a considerable distance, on both sides; on the east, the high ridges of the Westphalian mountains shut up the scene. The Rhine, which frequently swept near the road, shewed a broad surface, though shrunk within its sandy shores by the dryness of the season. Not a single vessel animated its current, which was here tame and smooth, though often interrupted by sands, that rose above its level.

HOOG-

HOOGSTRASS.

THE next town was Hoogſtraſs, a poſt ſtation, fifteen miles from Xanten, of which we ſaw little more than the inn, the other part of this ſmall place being out of the road. A large houſe, which might have been eaſily made convenient, and was really not without plenty, confirmed our notion, that, at the poſt ſtages, there would always be ſome accommodation. We dined here, and were well attended. The landlord, a young man who had ſerved in the army of the country, and appeared by his dreſs to have gained ſome promotion, was very induſtrious in the houſe, during this interval of his other employments.

The next ſtage was of eighteen miles, which make a German poſt and an half; and, during this ſpace, we paſſed by only one town, Ordingen, or Urdingen, the greatest part of which spread between the road and the Rhine.

Towards evening, the country became more woody, and the slender spires of convents frequently appeared, sheltered in their groves and surrounded by corn lands of their own domain. One of these, nearer to the road, was a noble mansion, and, with its courts, offices and gardens, spread over a considerable space. A summer-house, built over the garden wall, had no windows towards the road, but there were several small apertures, which looked upon it and beyond to a large tract of inclosed wood, the property of the convent.

NEUSS.

Soon after sun-set, we came to Neuss, which, as it is a post town, and was mentioned as far off as Xanten, we had been sure would afford a comfortable lodging, whether there were any vestiges, or not, of its ancient and modern history. The view of it, at some little distance, did not altogether contradict this notion, for it stands upon a gentle ascent, and the spires of several convents might justly give ideas of a considerable town to those, who had not learned how slightly such symptoms are to be attended to in Germany.

On each side of the gate, cannon balls of various sizes remain in the walls. Within, you enter immediately into a close street of high, but dirty stone houses, from which you expect to escape presently, supposing it to be only some wretched quarter, appropriated to disease and misfortune. You see no passengers, but, at the door of every house, an haggard group of men. and women stare upon you with looks of hungry rage, rather than curiosity, and their gaunt figures excite, at first, more fear than pity. Continuing to look for the better quarter, and to pass between houses, that seem to have been left after a siege and never entered since, the other gate of the town at length appears, which you would rather pass at midnight than stop at any place yet perceived. Within a small distance of the gate, there is, however, a house with a wider front, and windows of unshattered glass and walls not quite as black as the others, which is known to be the inn only because the driver stops there, for, according to the etiquette of sullenness in Germany, the people of the house make no shew of receiving you.

If

If it had not already appeared, that there was no other inn, you might learn it from the manners of the two hoſteſſes and their ſervants. Some ſort of accommodation is, however, to be had; and thoſe, who have been longer from the civilities and aſſiduities of ſimilar places in England, may, by more ſubmiſſion and more patience, obtain it ſooner than we did. By theſe means they may reduce all their difficulties into one, that of determining whether the windows ſhall be open or ſhut; whether they will endure the cloſeneſs of the rooms, or will admit air, loaded with the feculence of putrid kennels, that ſtagnate along the whole town.

This is the *Noveſium* of Tacitus, the entrance of the thirteenth legion into which he relates, at a time when the Rhine, *incognita illi cælo ſiccitate*, became *vix navium patiens*, and which VOCULA was ſoon after compelled to ſurrender by the treachery of other leaders and the corruption of his army, whom he addressed, just before his murder, in the fine speech, beginning, " *Nunquam apud vos verba feci, aut pro vobis folicitior, aut pro me fecurior* ; a passage so near to the *cunctifque timentem, fecurumque fui*, by which LUCAN describes CATO, that it must be supposed to have been inspired by it.

This place stood a siege, for twelve months, against 60,000 men, commanded by CHARLES the BOLD, Duke of Burgundy, and succeeded in its resistance. But, in 1586, when it held out for GEBHERT DE TRUSCHES, an Elector of Cologne, expelled by his Chapter, for having married, it was the scene of a dreadful calamity. FARNESE, the Spanish General, who had just taken Venlo, marched against it with an army, enraged at having lost the plunder of that place by a capitulation. When the inhabitants of Neuss were upon the point of surrendering

surrendering it, upon similar terms, the army, resolving not to lose another prey of blood and gold, rushed to the assault, set fire to the place, and murdered all the inhabitants, except a few women and children, who took refuge in two churches, which alone were saved from the flames.

When the first shock of the surprise, indignation and pity, excited by the mention of such events, is overcome, we are, of course, anxious to ascertain whether the perpetrators of them were previously distinguished by a voluntary entrance into situations, that could be supposed to mark their characters. This was the army of Philip the Second. The soldiers were probably, for the most part, forced into the service. The officers, of whom only two are related to have opposed the massacre, could not have been so.

What was then the previous distinction of the officers of Philip the Second? But

it

it is not proper to enter into a discussion here of the nature of their employment.

Neuss was rebuilt, on the same spot; the situation being convenient for an intercourse with the eastern shore of the Rhine, especially with Dusseldorff, to which it is nearly opposite. The ancient walls were partly restored by the French, in 1602. One of the churches, spared by the Spaniards, was founded by a daughter of CHARLEMAGNE, in the ninth century, and is now attached to the Chapter of Noble Ladies of St. Quirin; besides which there are a Chapter of Canons, and five or six convents in the place.

COLOGNE.

FROM Neuss hither we passed through a deep, sandy road, that sometimes wound near the Rhine, the shores of which were

were yet low and the water tame and shallow. There were no veffels upon it, to give one ideas either of the commerce, or the population of its banks.

The country, for the greater part of twenty miles, was a flat of corn' lands; but, within a fhort diftance of Cologne, a gentle rife affords a view of the whole city, whofe numerous towers and fteeples had before appeared, and of the extenfive plains, that fpread round it. In the fouthern perfpective of thefe, at the diftance of about eight leagues, rife the fantaftic forms of what are called the Seven Mountains; weftward, are the cultivated hills, that extend towards Flanders; and, eaftward, over the Rhine, the diftant mountains, that run through feveral countries of interior Germany. Over the wild and gigantic features of the Seven Mountains dark thunder mifts foon fpread an awful obfcurity, and heightened the expectation, which

this

this glimpse of them had awakened, concerning the scenery we were approaching.

The appearance of Cologne, at the distance of one, or two miles, is not inferior to the conception, which a traveller may have already formed of one of the capitals of Germany, should his mind have obeyed that almost universal illusion of fancy, which dresses up the images of places unseen, as soon as much expectation, or attention is directed towards them. The air above is crowded with the towers and spires of churches and convents, among which the cathedral, with its huge, unfinished mass, has a striking appearance. The walls are also high enough to be observed, and their whole inclosure seems, at a distance, to be thickly filled with buildings.

We should have known ourselves to be in the neighbourhood of some place larger than usual, from the sight of two, or three carriages, at once, on the road; nearly the

first

first we had seen in Germany. There is besides some shew of labour in the adjoining villages; but the sallow countenances and miserable air of the people prove, that it is not a labour beneficial to them. The houses are only the desolated homes of these villagers; for there is not one that can be supposed to belong to any prosperous inhabitant of the city, or to afford the coveted stillness, in which the active find an occasional reward, and the idle a perpetual misery.

A bridge over a dry fossé leads to the northern gate, on each side of which a small modern battery defends the ancient walls. The city is not fortified, according to any present sense of the term, but is surrounded by these walls and by a ditch, of which the latter, near the northern gate, serves as a sort of kitchen garden to the inhabitants.

Before passing the inner gate, a soldier demanded our names, and we shewed our passport,

paſſport, for the firſt time; but, as the inquiſitor did not underſtand French, in which language paſſports from England are written, it was handed to his comrades, who formed a circle about our chaiſe, and began, with leaden looks, to ſpell over the paper. Some talked, in the mean time, of examining the baggage; and the money, which we gave to prevent this, being in various pieces and in Pruſſian coin, which is not perfectly underſtood here, the whole party turned from the paſſport, counting and eſtimating the money in the hand of their collector, as openly as if it had been a legal tribute. When this was done and they had heard, with ſurpriſe, that we had not determined where to lodge, being inclined to take the pleaſanteſt inn, we wrote our names in the corporal's dirty book, and were allowed to drive, under a dark tower, into the city.

Inſtantly, the narrow ſtreet, gloomy houſes,

houses, stagnant kennels and wretchedly looking people reminded us of the horrors of Neuss. The lower windows of these prison-like houses are so strongly barricadoed, that we had supposed the first two, or three, to be really parts of a gaol; but it soon appeared, that this profusion of heavy iron work was intended to exclude, not to confine, robbers. A succession of narrow streets, in which the largest houses were not less disgusting than the others for the filthiness of their windows, doorways and massy walls, continued through half the city. In one of these streets, or lanes, the postillion stopped at the door of an inn, which he said was the best; but the suffocating air of the street rendered it unnecessary to enquire, whether, contrary to appearances, there could be any accommodation within, and, as we had read of many squares, or market-places, he was desired to stop at an inn, situated in one of these. Thus we came to the Hotel de Prague,

Prague, a large straggling building, said to be not worse than the others, for wanting half its furniture, and probably superior to them, by having a landlord of better than German civility.

Having counted from our windows the spires of ten, or twelve churches, or convents, we were at leisure to walk farther into the city, and to look for the spacious squares, neat streets, noble public buildings and handsome houses, which there could be no doubt must be found in an Imperial and Electoral city, seated on the Rhine, at a point where the chief roads from Holland and Flanders join those of Germany, treated by all writers as a considerable place, and evidently by its situation capable of becoming a sort of *emporium* for the three countries. The spot, into which our inn opened, though a parallelogram of considerable extent, bordered by lime trees, we passed quickly through, perceiving, that the

houses

houses on all its sides were mean buildings, and therefore such as could not deserve the attention in the Imperial and Electoral city of Cologne. There are streets from each angle of this place, and we pursued them all in their turn, narrow, winding and dirty as they are, pestilent with kennels, gloomy from the height and blackness of the houses, unadorned by any public buildings, except the churches, that were grand, or by one private dwelling, that appeared to be clean, with little shew of traffic and less of passengers, either busy, or gay, till we saw them ending in other streets still worse, or concluded by the gates of the city. One of them, indeed, led through a market-place, in which the air is free from the feculence of the streets, but which is inferior to the other opening in space, and not better surrounded by buildings.

" These diminutive observations seem to take away something from the dignity of writing,

writing, and therefore are never communicated, but with hesitation, and a little fear of abasement and contempt *." And it is not only because they take away something from the dignity of writing, that such observations are withheld. To be thought capable of commanding more pleasures and preventing more inconveniences than others is a too general passport to respect ;. and, in the ordinary affairs of life, for one, that will shew somewhat less prosperity than he has, in order to try who will really respect him, thousands exert themselves to assume an appearance of more, which they might know can procure only the mockery of esteem for themselves, and the reality of it for their supposed conditions. Authors are not always free from a willingness to receive the fallacious sort of respect, that attaches to accidental circumstances, for the real sort, of which it would be more reasonable to be

* Dr. Samuel Johnson.

proud.

proud. A man, relating part of the hiftory of his life, which is always neceffarily done by a writer of travels, does not choofe to fhew that his courfe could lie through any fcenes deficient of delights; or that, if it did, he was not enough elevated by his friends, importance, fortune, fame, or bufinefs, to be incapable of obferving them minutely. The curiofities of cabinets and of courts are, therefore, exactly defcribed, and as much of every occurrence as does not fhew the relater moving in any of the plainer walks of life; but the difference between the ftock of phyfical comforts in different countries, the character of conditions, if the phrafe may be ufed, fuch as it appears in the ordinary circumftances of refidence, drefs, food, cleanlinefs, opportunities of relaxation; in fhort, the information, which all may gain, is fometimes left to be gained by all, not from the book, but from travel. A writer, iffuing into the world,

world, makes up what he mistakes for his best appearance, and is continually telling his happiness, or shewing his good-humour, as people in a promenade always smile, and always look round to observe whether they are seen smiling. The politest salutation of the Chinese, when they meet, is, " Sir, prosperity is painted on your countenance;" or, " your whole air announces your felicity;" and the writers of travels, especially since the censure thrown upon SMOLLET, seem to provide, that their prosperity shall be painted on their volumes, and all their observations announce their felicity.

Cologne, though it bears the name of the Electorate, by which it is surrounded, is an imperial city; and the Elector, as to temporal affairs, has very little jurisdiction within it. The government has an affectation of being formed upon the model of Republican Rome; a form certainly not worthy

worthy of imitation, but which is as much disgraced by this burlesque of it, as ancient statues are by the gilding and the wigs, with which they are said to be sometimes arrayed by modern hands. There is a senate of forty-nine persons, who, being returned at different times of the year, are partly nominated by the remaining members, and partly chosen by twenty-two tribes of burgesses, or rather by so many companies of traders. Of six burgomasters, two are in office every third year, and, when these appear in public, they are preceded by LICTORS, bearing *fasces*, surmounted by their *own arms!* Each of the tribes, or companies, has a President, and the twenty-two Presidents form a Council, which is authorised to enquire into the conduct of the Senate: but the humbleness of the burgesses in their individual condition has virtually abolished all this scheme of a political constitution. Without some of the intelligence and personal independence, which are but little consistent with the general poverty and indolence of German traders, nothing but the forms of any constitution can be preserved, long after the virtual destruction of it has been meditated by those in a better condition. The greater part of these companies of traders having, in fact, no trade which can place them much above the rank of menial servants to their rich customers, the design, that their Council shall check the Senate, and the Senate direct the Burgomasters, has now, of course, little effect. And this, or a still humbler condition, is that of several cities in Germany, called free and independent, in which the neighbouring sovereigns have scarcely less authority, though with something more of circumstance, than in their own dominions.

The constitution of Cologne permits, indeed, some direct interference of the Elector;

tor; for the Tribunal of Appeal, which is the supreme court of law, is nominated by him: he has otherwise no direct power within the city; and, being forbidden to reside there more than three days successively, he does not even retain a palace, but is contented with a suite of apartments, reserved for his use at an inn. That this exclusion is no punishment, those, who have ever passed two days at Cologne, will admit; and it can tend very little to lessen his influence, for the greatest part of his personal expenditure must reach the merchants of the place; and the officers of several of his territorial jurisdictions make part of the inhabitants. His residences, with which he is remarkably well provided, are at Bonn; at Bruhl, a palace between Cologne and that place; at Poppelsdorff, which is beyond it; at Herzogs Freud, an hunting seat; and in Munster, of which he is the Bishop.

The duties of customs and excise are imposed by the magistrates of the city, and these enable them to pay their contributions to the Germanic fund; for, though such cities are formally independent of the neighbouring princes and nobility, they are not so of the general laws or expences of the empire, in the Diet of which they have some small share, forty-nine cities being allowed to send two representatives, and thus to have two votes out of an hundred and thirty-six. These duties, of both sorts, are very high at Cologne; and the first form a considerable part of the interruptions, which all the States upon the Rhine give to the commerce of that river. Here also commodities, intended to be carried beyond the city by water, must be re-shipped; for, in order to provide cargoes for the boatmen of the place, vessels from the lower parts of the Rhine are not allowed to ascend beyond Cologne, and those from the higher parts cannot

cannot defcend it farther. They may, indeed, reload with other cargoes for their return; and, as they conftantly do fo, the Cologne boatmen are not much benefited by the regulation; but the transfer of the goods employs fome hands, fubjects them better to the infpection of the cuftomhoufe officers, and makes it neceffary for the merchants of places, on both fides, trading with each other, to have intermediate correfpondents here. Yet, notwithftanding all this aggreffion upon the freedom of trade, Cologne is lefs confiderable as a port, than fome Dutch towns, never mentioned in a book, and is inferior, perhaps, to half the minor feaports in England. We could not find more than thirty veffels of burthen againft the quay, all mean and ill-built, except the Dutch, which are very large, and, being conftructed purpofely for a tedious navigation, contain apartments upon the deck for the family of the fkipper, well furnifhed,

and

and so commodious as to have four or five sashed windows on each side, generally gay with flower-pots. Little flower-gardens, too, sometimes formed upon the roof of the cabin, increase the domestic comforts of the skipper; and the neatness of his vessel can, perhaps, be equalled only by that of a Dutch house. In a time of perfect peace, there is no doubt more traffic; but, from what we saw of the general means and occasions of commerce in Germany, we cannot suppose it to be much reduced by war. Wealthy and commercial countries may be injured immensely by making war either for Germany or against it; by too much friendship or too much enmity; but Germany itself cannot be proportionately injured with them, except when it is the scene of actual violence. Englishmen, who feel, as they always must, the love of their own country much increased by the view of others, should be induced, at every step,

to

to wish, that there may be as little political intercourse as possible, either of friendship or enmity, between the blessings of their Island and the wretchedness of the Continent.

Our inn had formerly been a convent, and was in a part of the town where such societies are more numerous than elsewhere. At five o'clock, on the Sunday after our arrival, the bells of churches and convents began to sound on all sides, and there was scarcely any entire intermission of them till evening. The places of public amusement, chiefly a sort of tea-gardens, were then set open, and, in many streets, the sound of music and dancing was heard almost as plainly as that of the bells had been before; a disgusting excess of licentiousness, which appeared in other instances, for we heard, at the same time, the voices of a choir on one side of the street, and the noise of a billiard table on the other. Near the

the inn, this contraſt was more obſervable. While the ſtrains of revelry aroſe from an adjoining garden, into which our windows opened, a pauſe in the muſic allowed us to catch ſome notes of the veſper ſervice, performing in a convent of the order of Clariſſe, only three or four doors beyond. Of the ſevere rules of this ſociety we had been told in the morning. The members take a vow, not only to renounce the world, but their deareſt friends, and are never after permitted to ſee even their fathers or mothers, though they may ſometimes converſe with the latter from behind a curtain. And, leſt ſome lingering remains of filial affection ſhould tempt an unhappy nun to lift the veil of ſeparation between herſelf and her mother, ſhe is not allowed to ſpeak even with her, but in the preſence of the abbeſs. Accounts of ſuch horrible perverſions of human reaſon make the blood thrill and the teeth chatter. Their fathers they can never

ſpeak

speak to, for no man is suffered to be in any part of the convent used by the sisterhood, nor, indeed, is admitted beyond the gate, except when there is a necessity for repairs, when all the votaries of the order are previously secluded. It is not easily, that a cautious mind becomes convinced of the existence of such severe orders; when it does, astonishment at the artificial miseries, which the ingenuity of human beings forms for themselves by seclusion, is as boundless as at the other miseries, with which the most trivial vanity and envy so frequently pollute the intercourses of social life. The poor nuns, thus nearly entombed during their lives, are, after death, tied upon a board, in the clothes they die in, and, with only their veils thrown over the face, are buried in the garden of the convent.

During this day, Trinity Sunday, processions were passing on all sides, most of them attended by some sort of martial music.

music. Many of the parishes, of which there are nineteen, paraded with their officers; and the burgesses, who are distributed into eight corps, under a supposition that they could and would defend the city, if it was attacked, presented their captains at the churches. The host accompanied all these processions. A party of the city guards followed, and forty or fifty persons out of uniform, the representatives probably of the burgesses, who are about six thousand, succeeded. Besides the guards, there was only one man in uniform, who, in the burlesque dress of a drum-major, entertained the populace by a kind of extravagant marching dance, in the middle of the procession. Our companion would not tell us that this was the captain.

The cathedral, though unfinished, is conspicuous, amongst a great number of churches, for the dignity of some detached features, that shew part of the vast design formed

formed for the whole. It was begun, in 1248, by the Elector Conrad, who is related, in an hexameter infcription over a gate, to have laid the firft ftone himfelf. In 1320, the choir was finifhed, and the workmen continued to be employed upon the other parts in 1499, when of two towers, deftined to be 580 feet above the roof, one had rifen 21 feet, and the other 150 feet, according to the meafurement mentioned in a printed defcription. We did not learn at what period the defign of completing the edifice was abandoned; but the original founder lived to fee all the treafures expended, which he had collected for the purpofe. In its prefent ftate, the inequality of its vaft towers renders it a ftriking object at a confiderable diftance; and, from the large unfilled area around it, the magnificence of its Gothic architecture, efpecially of fome parts, which have not been joined to the reft, and appear to be the ruined

ruined remains, rather than the commencement of a work, is viewed with awful delight.

In the interior of the cathedral, a fine choir leads to an altar of black marble, raised above several steps, which, being free from the incongruous ornaments usual in Romish churches, is left to impress the mind by its majestic plainness. The tall painted windows above, of which there are six, are superior in richness of colouring and design to any we ever saw; beyond even those in the Chapter-house at York, and most resembling the very fine ones in the cathedral of Canterbury. The nave is deformed by a low wooden roof, which appears to have been intended only as a temporary covering, and should certainly be succeeded by one of equal dignity to the vast columns placed for its support, whether the other parts of the original design can ever be completed or not.

By

By some accident we did not see the tomb of the three kings of Jerusalem, whose bodies are affirmed to have been brought here from Milan in 1162, when the latter city was destroyed by the Emperor Frederic Barbarossa. Their boasted treasures of golden crowns and diamonds pass, of course, without our estimation.

A description of the churches in Cologne, set out with good antiquarian minuteness, would fill volumes. The whole number of churches, chapters and chapels, which last are by far the most numerous, is not less than eighty, and none are without an history of two or three centuries. They are all opened on Sundays; and we can believe, that the city may contain, as is asserted, 40,000 souls, for nearly all that we saw were well attended. In one, indeed, the congregation consisted only of two or three females, kneeling at a great distance from the altar, with an appearance of the utmost intentness upon the service, and abstraction from the noise of the processions, that could be easily heard within. They were entirely covered with a loose black drapery; whether for penance, or not, we did not hear. In the cathedral, a figure in the same attitude was rendered more interesting by her situation beneath the broken arches and shattered fret-work of a painted window, through which the rays of the sun scarcely penetrated to break the shade she had chosen.

Several of the chapels are not much larger than an ordinary apartment, but they are higher, that the nuns of some adjoining convent may have a gallery, where, veiled from observation by a lawn curtain, their voices often mingle sweetly with the choir. There are thirty-nine convents of women and nineteen of men, which are supposed to contain about fifteen hundred persons. The chapters, of which some are

noble

noble and extremely opulent, support nearly four hundred more; and there are said to be, upon the whole, between two and three thousand persons, under religious denominations, in Cologne. Walls of convents and their gardens appear in every street, but do not attract notice, unless, as frequently happens, their bell sounds while you are passing. Some of their female inhabitants may be seen in various parts of the city, for there is an order, the members of which are employed, by rotation, in teaching children and attending the sick. Those of the noble chapters are little more confined than if they were with their own families, being permitted to visit their friends, to appear at balls and promenades, to wear what dresses they please, except when they chaunt in the choir, and to quit the chapter, if the offer of an acceptable marriage induces their families to authorise it; but their own admission into the chapter proves them to be noble by sixteen quarterings, or four generations, and the offer must be from a person of equal rank, or their descendants could not be received into similar chapters; an important circumstance in the affairs of the German noblesse.

Some of these ladies we saw in the church of their convent. Their habits were remarkably graceful; robes of lawn and black silk flowed from the shoulder, whence a quilled ruff, somewhat resembling that of Queen Elizabeth's time, spread round the neck. The hair was in curls, without powder, and in the English fashion. Their voices were peculiarly sweet, and they sung the responses with a kind of plaintive tenderness, that was extremely interesting.

The Jesuits' church is one of the grandest in Cologne, and has the greatest display of paintings over its numerous altars, as well as of marble pillars. The churches of the chapters are, for the most part, very large,

large, and endowed with the richeſt ornaments, which are, however, not ſhewn to the public, except upon days of fête. We do not remember to have ſeen that of the chapter of St. Urſula, where heads and other relics are ſaid to be handed to you from ſhelves, like books in a library; nor that of the convent of Jacobins, where ſome MSS. and other effects of Albert the Great, biſhop of Ratiſbon, are among the treaſures of the monks.

Oppoſite to the Jeſuits' church was an hoſpital for wounded ſoldiers, ſeveral of whom were walking in the court yard before it, half-clothed in dirty woollen, through which the bare arms of many appeared. Sickneſs and neglect had ſubdued all the ſymptoms of a ſoldier; and it was impoſſible to diſtinguiſh the wounded French from the others, though we were aſſured that ſeveral of that nation were in the crowd. The windows of the hoſpital were filled

filled with figures still more wretched. There was a large assemblage of spectators, who looked as if they were astonished to see, that war is compounded of something else, besides the glories, of which it is so easy to be informed.

The soldiery of Cologne are under the command of the magistrates, and are employed only within the gates of the city. The whole body does not exceed an hundred and fifty, whom we saw reviewed by their colonel, in the place before the Hotel de Prague. The uniform is red, faced with white. The men wear whiskers, and affect an air of ferocity, but appear to be mostly invalids, who have grown old in their guard-houses.

Protestants, though protected in their persons, are not allowed the exercise of their religion within the walls of the city, but have a chapel in a village on the other side of the Rhine. As some of the chief merchants,

merchants, and thofe who are moft ufeful to the inhabitants, are of the reformed church, they ventured lately to requeft that they might have a place of worfhip within the city; but they received the common anfwer, which oppofes all fort of improvement, religious or civil, that, though the privilege in itfelf might be juftly required, it could not be granted, becaufe they would then think of afking fomething more.

The government of Cologne in ecclefiaftical affairs is with the Elector, as archbifhop, and the Chapter as his council. In civil matters, though the city conftitution is of little effect, the real power is not fo conftantly with him as might be fuppofed; thofe, who have influence, being fometimes out of his intereft. Converfation, as we were told, was fcarcely lefs free than in Holland, where there is juftly no oppofition to any opinion, however improper, or abfurd, except from the reafon of thofe, who

hear

hear it. On that account, and becaufe of its eafy intercourfe with Bruffels and Spa, this city is fomewhat the refort of ftrangers, by whom fuch converfation is, perhaps, chiefly carried on; but thofe muft come from very wretched countries who can find pleafure in a refidence at Cologne.

Amongft the public buildings muft be reckoned the Theatre, of which we did not fee the infide, there being no performance, during our ftay, except on Sunday. This, it feems, may be opened, without offence to the Magiftrates, though a proteftant church may not. It ftands in a row of fmall houfes, from which it is diftinguifhed only by a painted front, once tawdry and now dirty, with the infcription, " *Mufis Gratiifque decentibus.*" The Town-houfe is an awkward and irregular ftone building. The arfenal, which is in one of the narroweft ftreets, we fhould have paffed, without notice, if it had not been pointed out to us.

us. As a building, it is nothing more than such as might be formed out of four or five of the plainest houses laid into one. Its contents are said to be chiefly antient arms, of various fashions and sizes, not very proper for modern use.

BONN.

AFTER a stay of nearly three tedious days, we left Cologne for Bonn, passing through an avenue of limes, which extends from one place to the other, without interruption, except where there is a small half way village. The distance is not less than eighteen miles, and the diversified culture of the plains, through which it passes, is unusually grateful to the eye, after the dirty buildings of Cologne and the long uniformity of corn lands in the approach to it.

it. Vines cover a great part of these plains, and are here first seen in Germany, except, indeed, within the walls of Cologne itself, which contain many large inclosures, converted from gardens and orchards into well sheltered vineyards. The vines reminded us of English hop plants, being set, like them, in rows, and led round poles to various heights, though all less than that of hops. Corn, fruit or herbs were frequently growing between the rows, whose light green foliage mingled beautifully with yellow wheat and larger patches of garden plantations, that spread, without any inclosures, to the sweeping Rhine, on the left. Beyond, appeared the blue ridges of Westphalian mountains. On the right, the plains extend to a chain of lower and less distant hills, whose skirts are covered with vines and summits darkened with thick woods.

The Elector's palace of Bruhl is on the right hand of the road, at no great distance;
but

but we were not told, till afterwards, of the magnificent architecture and furniture, which ought to have attracted our curiosity.

On a green and circular, hill, near the Rhine, ſtands the Benedictine abbey of Siegbourg, one of the firſt picturefque objects of the rich approach to Bonn; and, further on, the caſtle-like towers of a convent of noble ladies; both focieties celebrated for their wealth and the pleafantneſs of their fituations, which command extenfive profpects over the country, on each fide of the river. As we drew near Bonn, we frequently caught, between the trees of the avenue, imperfect, but awakening glimpfes of the pointed mountains beyond; contraſted with the folemn grandeur of which was the beauty of a round woody hill, apparently feparated from them only by the Rhine and crowned with the fpire of a comely convent. Bonn, with tall flender ſteeples and the trees of its ramparts, thus

backed

backed by sublime mountains, looks well, as you approach it from Cologne, though neither its noble palace, nor the Rhine, which washes its walls, are seen from hence. We were asked our names at the gate, but had no trouble about passports, or baggage. A long and narrow street leads from thence to the market-place, not disgusting you either with the gloom, or the dirt of Cologne, though mean houses are abundantly intermixed with the others, and the best are far from admirable. The *physiognomy of the place*, if one may use the expression, is wholesome, though humble. By the recommendation of a Dutch merchant, we went to an inn in another street, branching from the market-place, and found it the cleanest, since we had left Holland.

Bonn may be called the political capital of the country, the Elector's Court being held only there; and, what would not be expected, this has importance enough to command

command the refidence of an agent from almoft every Power in Europe. The prefent Elector being the uncle of the Emperor, this attention is, perhaps, partly paid, with the view, that it may be felt at the Court of Vienna. Even Ruffia is not unreprefented in this miniature State.

The Elector's palace is, in point of grandeur, much better fitted to be the fcene of diplomatic ceremonies, than thofe of many greater Sovereigns; and it is fitted alfo for better than diplomatic purpofes, being placed before fome of the moft ftriking of nature's features, of which it is nearly as worthy an ornament as art can make. It is feated on the weftern bank of the Rhine, the general courfe of which it fronts, though it forms a confiderable angle with the part immediately neareft. The firft emotion, on perceiving it, being that of admiration, at its vaftnefs, the wonder is, of courfe, equal, with which you difcover, that it is only

part

part of a greater defign. It confifts of a centre and an eaftern wing, which are completed, and of a weftern wing, of which not half is yet raifed. The extent from eaft to weft is fo great, that, if we had enquired the meafurement, we fhould have been but little affifted in giving an idea of the fpectacle, exhibited by fo immenfe a building.

It is of ftone, of an architecture, perhaps, not adequate to the grandeur of its extent, but which fills no part with unfuitable, or inelegant ornaments. Along the whole garden front, which is the chief, a broad terrace fupports a promenade and an orangery of noble trees, occafionally refrefhed by fountains, that, ornamented with ftatues, rife from marble bafons. An arcade through the centre of the palace leads to this terrace, from whence the profpect is ftrikingly beautiful and fublime. The eye paffes over the green lawn of the garden and a tract of

level

level country to the groupe, called the Seven Mountains, broken, rocky and abrupt towards their summits, yet sweeping finely near their bases, and uniting with the plains by long and gradual descents, that spread round many miles. The nearest is about a league and a half off. We saw them under the cloudless sky of June, invested with the mistiness of heat, which softening their rocky points, and half veiling their recesses, left much for the imagination to supply, and gave them an aërial appearance, a faint tint of silvery grey, that was inexpressibly interesting. The Rhine, that winds at their feet, was concealed from us by the garden groves, but from the upper windows of the palace it is seen in all its majesty.

On the right from this terrace, the smaller palace of Poppelsdorff terminates a long avenue of limes and chesnut trees, that communicates with both buildings, and above are the hill and the convent. *Sancta Crucis,*

Crucis, the latter looking out from among firs and shrubby steeps. From thence the western horizon is bounded by a range of hills, clothed to their summits with wood. The plain, that extends between these and the Rhine, is cultivated with vines and corn, and the middle distance is marked by a pyramidal mountain, darkened by wood and crowned with the tower and walls of a ruined castle.

The gardens of the palace are formally laid out in straight walks and alleys of cut trees; but the spacious lawn between these gives fine effect to the perspective of the distant mountains; and the bowery walks, while they afford refreshing shelter from a summer sun, allow partial views of the palace and the romantic landscape.

It was the Elector Joseph Clement, the same who repaired the city, left in a ruinous state by the siege of 1703, under the Duke of Marlborough, that built this magnificent

nificent refidence. There are in it many fuites of ftate rooms and every fort of apartment ufual in the manfions of Sovereigns; faloons of audience and ceremony, a library, a cabinet of natural hiftory and a theatre. Though thefe are readily opened to ftrangers, we are to confefs, that we did not fee them, being prevented by the attentions of thofe, whofe civilities gave them a right to command us, while their fituations enabled them to point out the beft occupation of our time. The hall of the Grand Mafter of the Teutonic Order, ornamented with portraits of all the grand mafters, we are, however, forry to have neglected even for the delights of Poppelfdorff, which we were prefently fhewn.

Leaving the palace, we paffed through the garden, on the right, to a fine avenue of turf, nearly a mile long, bordered by alleys of tall trees, and fo wide, that the late Elector had defigned to form a canal

in the middle of it, for an opportunity of paffing between his palaces, by land, or water, as he might wifh. The palace of Poppelfdorff terminates the perfpective of this avenue. It is a fmall building, furrounded by its gardens, in a tafte not very good, and remarkable chiefly for the pleafantnefs of its fituation. An arcade, encompaffing a court in the interior, communicates with all the apartments on the ground floor, which is the principal, and with the gardens, on the eaftern fide of the chateau. The entrance is through a fmall hall, decorated with the enfigns of hunting, and round nearly the whole arcade ftags' heads are placed, at equal diftances. Thefe have remained here, fince the reign of Clement Auguftus, the founder of the palace, who died in 1761; and they exhibit fome part of the hiftory of his life; for, under each, is an infcription, relating the events and date of the hunt, by which he
killed

killed it. There are twenty-three such ornaments.

The greatest part of the furniture had been removed, during the approach of the French, in 1792; and the Archduchess Maria Christina, to whom the Elector, her brother, had lent the chateau, was now very far from sumptuously accommodated. On this account, she passed much of her time, at Goodesberg, a small watering place in the neighbourhood. After her retreat from Brussels, in consequence of the advances of the French in the same year, she had accompanied her husband, the Duke of Saxe Teschen, into Saxony; but, since his appointment to the command of the Emperor's army of the Upper Rhine, her residence had been established in the dominions of her brother.

We were shewn through her apartments, which she had left for Goodesberg, a few hours before. On the table of her sitting room lay the fragments of a painted cross, composed of small pieces, like our dissected maps, the putting of which together exercises ingenuity and passes, perhaps, for a sort of piety. The attendant said, that it served to pass the time; but it cannot be supposed, that rank and fortune have so little power to bestow happiness, as that their possessors should have recourse to such means of lightening the hours of life.

On another table, was spread a map of all the countries, then included in the Theatre of War, and on it a box, filled with small pieces of various coloured wax, intended to mark the positions of the different armies. These were of many shades; for the Archduchess, who is said to be conversant with military affairs and to have descended to the firing of bombs at the siege of Lisle, was able to distinguish the several corps of the allied armies, that were acting separately from each other. The positions were

were marked up to the lateſt accounts then public. The courſe of her thoughts was viſible from this chart, and they were intereſting to curioſity, being thoſe of the ſiſter of the late unfortunate Queen of France.

The walls of an adjoining cabinet were ornamented with drawings from the antique by the Archducheſs, diſpoſed upon a light ground and ſerving inſtead of tapeſtry.

The chapel is a rotunda, riſing into a dome, and, though ſmall, is ſplendid with painting and gilding. In the centre are four altars, formed on the four ſides of a ſquare pedeſtal, that ſupports a figure of our Saviour; but the beauty of this deſign is marred by the vanity of placing near each altar the ſtatue of a founder of the Teutonic order. The furniture of the Elector's gallery is of crimſon velvet and gold.

On another ſide of the chateau, we were ſhewn

shewn an apartment entirely covered with grotto work, and called the hall of shells; a curious instance of patient industry, having been completed by one man, during a labour of many years. Its situation in the middle of an inhabited mansion is unsuitable to the character of a grotto: but its coolness must render it a very convenient retreat; and the likenesses of animals, as well as the other forms, into which the shells are thrown, though not very elegant, are fanciful enough, especially as the ornaments of fountains, which play into several parts of the room.

Leaving the palace by the bridge of a moat, that nearly surrounds it, we passed through the pleasant village of Poppelsdorff, and ascended the hill SANCTÆ CRUCIS, called so from the convent of the same name, which occupies its summit. The road wound between thick woods; but we soon left it for a path, that led more immediately

diately to the summit, among shrubs and plantations of larch and fir, and which opened into easy avenues of turf, that sometimes allowed momentary views of other woody points and of the plains around. The turf was uncommonly fragrant and fine, abounding with plants, which made us regret the want of a Botanist's knowledge and pleasures. During the ascent, the peaked tops of the mountains of the Rhine, so often admired below, began to appear above a ridge of dark woods, very near us, in a contrast of hues, which was exquisitely fine. It was now near evening; the mistiness of heat was gone from the surface of these mountains, and they had assumed a blue tint so peculiar and clear, that they appeared upon the sky, like supernatural transparencies.

We had heard, at Bonn, of the Capuchins' courtesy, and had no hesitation to knock at their gate, after taking some rest in the portico of the church, from whence we looked down another side of the mountain, over the long plains between Bonn and Cologne. Having waited some time at the gate, during which many steps fled along the passage and the head of a monk appeared peeping through a window above, a servant admitted us into a parlour, adjoining the refectory, which appeared to have been just left. This was the first convent we had entered, and we could not help expecting to see more than others had described; an involuntary habit, from which few are free, and which need not be imputed to vanity, so long as the love of surprise shall be so visible in human pursuits. When the lay-brother had quitted us, to inform the superior of our request, not a footstep, or a voice approached, for near a quarter of an hour, and the place seemed as if uninhabited. Our curiosity had no indulgence within the room, which was of the utmost plainness, and that plainness free from any thing, that the most tractable imagination could suppose peculiar to a convent. At length, a monk appeared, who received us with infinite good humour, and with the ease which must have been acquired in more general society. His shaven head and black garments formed a whimsical contrast to the character of his person and countenance, which bore no symptoms of sorrow, or penance, and were, indeed, animated by an air of cheerfulness and intelligence, that would have become the happiest inhabitant of the gayest city.

Through some silent passages, in which he did not shew us a cell and we did not perceive another monk, we passed to the church, where the favour of several Electors has assisted the display of paintings, marble, sculpture, gold and silver, mingled and arranged with magnificent effect. Among these was the marble statue, brought from England,

England, at a great expence, and here called a reprefentation of St. Anne, who is faid to have found the Crofs. Our conductor feemed to be a man of good underftanding and defirous of being thought fo; a difpofition, which gave an awkwardnefs to his manner, when, in noticing a relic, he was obliged to touch upon fome unproved and unimportant tradition, peculiar to his church and not effential to the leaft article of our faith. His fenfe of decorum as a member of the convent feemed then to be ftruggling with his vanity, as a man.

But there are relics here, pretending to a connection with fome parts of chriftian hiftory, which it is fhocking to fee introduced to confideration by any means fo trivial and fo liable to ridicule. It is, indeed, wonderful, that the abfurd exhibitions, made in Romifh churches, fhould fo often be minutely defcribed, and dwelt upon in terms of ludicrous exultation by thofe, who
do

do not intend that moſt malignant of offences againſt human nature, the endeavour to excite a wretched vanity by ſarcaſm and jeſt, and to employ it in eradicating the comforts of religion. To ſuch writers, the probable miſchief of uniting with the mention of the moſt important divine doctrines the moſt ridiculous of human impoſitions ought to be apparent; and, as the riſk is unneceſſary in a Proteſtant country, why is it encountered? That perſons otherwiſe inclined ſhould adopt theſe topics is not ſurpriſing; the eaſieſt pretences to wit are found to be made by means of familiar alluſions to ſacred ſubjects, becauſe their neceſſary incongruity accompliſhes the greateſt part of what, in other caſes, muſt be done by wit itſelf; there will, therefore, never be an end of ſuch alluſions, till it is generally ſeen, that they are the reſources and ſymptoms of mean underſtandings, urged by the

feveriſh

feverish desire of an eminence, to which they feel themselves inadequate.

From the chapel we ascended to a tower of the convent, whence all the scattered scenes, of whose beauty, or sublimity, we had caught partial glimpses between the woods below, were collected into one vast landscape, and exhibited almost to a single glance. The point, on which the convent stands, commands the whole horizon. To the north, spread the wide plains, before seen, covered with corn, then just embrowned, and with vines and gardens, whose alternate colours formed a gay checker work with villages, convents and castles. The grandeur of this level was unbroken by any inclosures, that could seem to diminish its vastness. The range of woody heights, that bound it on the west, extend to the southward, many leagues beyond the hill *Sanctæ Crucis;* but the uniform and unbroken

unbroken ridges of diftant mountains, on the eaft, ceafe before the Seven Mountains rife above the Rhine in all their awful majefty. The bafes of the latter were yet concealed by the woody ridge near the convent, which gives fuch enchanting effect to their aërial points. The fky above them, was clear and glowing, unftained by the lighteft vapour; and thefe mountains ftill appeared upon it, like unfubftantial vifions. On the two higheft pinnacles we could juft diftinguifh the ruins of caftles, and, on a lower precipice, a building, which our reverend guide pointed out as a convent, dedicated to St. Bernard, giving us new occafion to admire the fine tafte of the monks in their choice of fituations.

Oppofite to the Seven Mountains, the plains of Goodefberg are fcreened by the chain of hills already mentioned, which begin in the neighbourhood of Cologne, and whofe woods, fpreading into France, there
affume

assume the name of the Forest of Ardennes. Within the recesses of these woods the Elector has a hunting-seat, almost every window of which opens upon a different alley, and not a stag can cross these without being seen from the chateau. It is melancholy to consider, that the most frequent motives of man's retirement among the beautiful recesses of nature, are only those of destroying the innocent animals that inhabit her shades. Strange! that her lovely scenes cannot soften his heart to milder pleasures, or elevate his fancy to nobler pursuits, and that he must still seek his amusement in scattering death among the harmless and the happy.

As we afterwards walked in the garden of the convent, the greater part of which was planted with vines, the monk further exhibited his good humour and liberality. He enquired concerning the events of the war, of which he appeared to know the latest;

lateſt; ſpoke of his friends in Cologne and other places; drew a ludicrous picture of the effect which would be produced by the appearance of a capuchin in London, and laughed immoderately at it. " There," ſaid he, " it would be ſuppoſed, that ſome harlequin was walking in a capuchin's dreſs to attract ſpectators for a pantomime; here nobody will follow him, leſt he ſhould lead them to church. Every nation has its way, and laughs at the ways of others. Conſidering the effects, which differences ſometimes have, there are few things more innocent than that ſort of laughter."

The garden was ſtored with fruits and the vegetable luxuries of the table, but was laid out with no attention to beauty, its inimitable proſpects having, as the good monk ſaid, rendered the ſociety careleſs of leſs advantages. After exchanging our thanks for his civilities againſt his thanks for the viſit, we deſcended to Poppelſdorff

by

by a steep road, bordered with firs and fragrant shrubs, which frequently opened to corn lands and vineyards, where peasants were busied in dressing the vines.

About a mile from Bonn is a garden, or rather nursery, to which they have given the name of *Vauxhall*. It is much more rural than that of London, being planted with thick and lofty groves, which, in this climate, are gratefully refreshing, during the summer-day, but are very pernicious in the evening, when the vapour, arising from the ground, cannot escape through the thick foliage. The garden is lighted up only on great festivals, or when the Elector or his courtiers give a ball in a large room built for the purpose. On some days, half the inhabitants of Bonn are to be seen in this garden, mingling in the promenade with the Elector and his nobility; but there were few visitors when we saw it. Count GIMNICH, the commander, who had surrendered

dered Mentz to the French, was the only perſon pointed out to us.

The road from hence to Bonn was laid out and planted with poplars at the expence of the Elector, who has a taſte for works of public advantage and ornament. His Grand-maſterſhip of the Teutonic Order renders his Court more frequented than thoſe of the other eccleſiaſtical Princes, the poſſeſſions of that Order being ſtill conſiderable enough to ſupport many younger brothers of noble families. Having paſſed his youth in the army, or at the courts of Vienna or Bruſ-ſels, he is alſo environed by friends, made before the vacancy of an eccleſiaſtical electorate induced him to change his profeſ-ſion; and the union of his three incomes, as Biſhop of Munſter, Grand Maſter and Elector, enables him to ſpend ſomething more than two hundred thouſand pounds annually. His experience and revenues are, in many reſpects, very uſefully employed.

Q To

To the nobility he affords an example of so much personal dignity, as to be able to reject many ostentatious customs, and to remove some of the ceremonial barriers, which men do not constantly place between themselves and their fellow-beings, except from some consciousness of personal weakness. All sovereigns, who have had any sense of their individual liberty and power, have shewn a readiness to remove such barriers; but not many have been able to effect so much as the Elector of Cologne against the chamberlains, pages, and other footmanry of their courts, who are always upon the *alerte* to defend the false magnificence that makes their offices seem necessary. He now enjoys many of the blessings, usual only in private stations; among others, that of conversing with great numbers of persons, not forced into his society by their rank, and of dispensing with much of that attendance, which would

render

GERMANY.

render his menial servants part of his company.

His secretary, Mr. Floret, whom we had the pleasure to see, gave us some accounts of the industry and carefulness of his private life, which he judiciously thought were better than any other panegyrics upon his master. His attention to the relief, employment and education of the poor, to the state of manufactures and the encouragement of talents, appears to be continual; and his country would soon have elapsed from the general wretchedness of Germany, if the exertions of three campaigns had not destroyed what thirty years of care and improvement cannot restore.

His residence at Bonn occasions expenditure enough to keep the people busy, but he has not been able to divert to it any part of the commerce, which, though it is of so little use at Cologne, is here spoken of

with

with some envy, and seems to be estimated above its amount. The town, which is much neater than the others in the electorate, and so pleasantly situated, that its name has been supposed to be formed from the Latin synonym for good, is ornamented by few public buildings, except the palace. What is called the University is a small brick building, used more as a school than a college, except that the masters are called professors. The principal church of four, which are within the walls, is a large building, distinguished by several spires, but not remarkable for its antiquity or beauty.

Many of the German powers retain some shew of a representative government, as to affairs of finance, and have States, by which taxes are voted. Those of the electorate of Cologne consist of four colleges, representing the clergy, nobility, knights and cities; the votes are given by colleges, so that the

inhabitants

inhabitants of the cities, if they elect their reprefentatives fairly, have one vote in four. Thefe States affemble at Bonn.

One of the privileges, which it is furprifing that the prefent Elector fhould retain, is that of grinding corn for the confumption of the whole town. His mill, like thofe of all the towns on the Rhine, is a floating one, moored in the river, which turns its wheel. Bread is bad at Bonn; but this oppreffive privilege is not entirely anfwerable for it, there being little better throughout the whole country. It generally appears in rolls, with glazed crufts, half hollow; the crumb not brown, but a fort of dirty white.

There are few cities in Germany without walls, which, when the dreadful fcience of war was lefs advanced than at prefent, frequently protected them againft large armies. Thefe are now fo ufelefs, that fuch cannon as are employed againft batteries could probably not be fired from them without shaking their foundations. The fortifications of Bonn are of this sort; and, though they were doubtless better, when the Duke of Marlborough arrived before them, it is wonderful that they should have sustained a regular siege, during which great part of the town was demolished. The electorate of Cologne is, indeed, so ill prepared for war, that it has not one town, which could resist ten thousand men for three days.

The inhabitants of Bonn, whenever they regret the loss of their fortifications, should be reminded of the three sieges, which, in the course of thirty years, nearly destroyed their city. Of these the first was in 1673, when the Elector had received a French garrison into it; but the resistance did not then continue many days. It was in this siege that the Prince of Orange, afterwards our honoured William the Third, had one of his few military successes. In 1689, the
 French,

GERMANY.

French, who had lately defended it, returned to attack it; and, before they could subdue the strong garrison left in it by the Elector of Brandenburg, the palace and several public buildings were destroyed. The third siege was commanded by the Duke of Marlborough, and continued from the 24th of April to the 16th of May, the French being then the defenders, and the celebrated Cohorn one of the assailants. It was not till fifteen years afterwards, that all the houses, demolished in this siege, could be restored by the efforts of the Elector Joseph.

The present Elector maintains, in time of peace, about eight hundred soldiers, which is the number of his contingent to the army of the Empire: in the present war he has supplied somewhat more than this allotment; and, when we were at Bonn, two thousand recruits were in training. His troops wear the general uniform of the Empire,

Empire, blue faced with red, which many of the Germanic sovereigns give only to their contingent troops, while those of their separate establishments are distinguished by other colours. The Austrian regiments are chiefly in white, faced with light blue, grey, or red; but the artillery are dressed, with very little shew, in a cloak speckled with light brown.

Bonn was one of the very few places in Germany, which we left with regret. It is endeared to the votaries of landscape by its situation in the midst of fruitful plains, in the presence of stupendous mountains, and on the bank of a river, that, in summer, is impelled by the dissolved snows of Switzerland, and, in winter, rolls with the accumulation of a thousand torrents from the rocks on its shores. It contained many inhabitants, who had the independence to aim at a just taste in morals and letters, in spite of the ill examples with which such countries

tries supply them; and, having the vices of the form of government, established in it, corrected by the moderation and immediate attention of the governor, it might be considered as a happy region in the midst of ignorance, injustice and misery, and remembered like the green spot, that, in an Arabian desert, cheers the senses and sustains the hopes of the weary traveller.

GOODESBERG.

THE ride from Bonn to this delightful village is only one league over a narrow plain, covered with corn and vineyards. On our right was the range of hills, before seen from the mountain SANC-TÆ CRUCIS, sweeping into frequent recesses, and starting forward into promontories, with inequalities, which gave exquisite richness

richness to the forest, that mantled from their bases to their utmost summits. Many a lurking village, with its slender grey steeple, peeped from among the woody skirts of these hills. On our left, the tremendous mountains, that bind the eastern shore of the Rhine, gradually lost their aërial complexion, as we approached them, and displayed new features and new enchantments; an ever-varying illusion, to which the transient circumstance of thunder clouds contributed. The sun-beams, streaming among these clouds, threw partial gleams upon the precipices, and, followed by dark shadows, gave surprising and inimitable effect to the natural colouring of the mountains, whose pointed tops we now discerned to be covered with dark heath, extended down their rocky sides, and mingled with the reddish and light yellow tints of other vegetation and the soil. It was delightful to watch the shadows sweeping over these steeps,

steeps, now involving them in deep obscurity, and then leaving them to the sun's rays, which brought out all their hues into vivid contrast.

Near Goodesberg, a small mountain, insulated, abrupt and pyramidal, rises from the plain, which it seems to terminate, and conceals the village, that lies along its southern skirt. This mountain, covered with vineyards and thick dwarf wood to its summit, where one high tower and some shattered walls appear, is a very interesting object.

At the entrance of the village, the road was obstructed by a great number of small carts, filled with soldiers apparently wounded. The line of their procession had been broken by some carriages, hastening with company to the ridotto at Goodesberg, and was not easily restored. Misery and festivity could scarcely be brought into closer contrast. We thought of Johnson's " many-coloured

coloured life," and of his picture, in the preface to Shakespeare, of cotemporary wretchedness and joy, when " the reveller is hastening to his wine, and the mourner is burying his friend." This was a procession of wounded French prisoners, chiefly boys, whose appearance had, indeed, led us to suspect their nation, before we saw the stamp of the *fasces*, and the words " *Republique Françoise*" upon the buttons of some, whom our driver had nearly overset. The few, that could raise themselves above the floor of their carts, shewed countenances yellow, or livid with sickness. They did not talk to their guards, nor did the latter shew any signs of exultation over them.

In a plain, beyond the village, a row of large houses, built upon one plan, and almost resembling a palace, form the little watering place of Goodesberg, which has been founded partly at the expence of the Elector, and partly by individuals under

his

his patronage. One of the houses was occupied by the Archduchess, his sister, and is often used by the Elector, who is extremely solicitous for the prosperity of the place. A large building at the end contains the public rooms, and is fitted up as an hotel.

The situation of this house is beautiful beyond any hope or power of description; for description, though it may tell that there are mountains and rocks, cannot paint the grandeur, or the elegance of outline, cannot give the effect of precipices, or draw the minute features, that reward the actual observer by continual changes of colour, and by varying their forms at every new choice of his position. Delightful Goodesberg! the sublime and beautiful of landscape, the charms of music, and the pleasures of gay and elegant society, were thine! The immediate unhappiness of war has now fallen upon thee; but, though the

graces

graces may have fled thee, thy terrible majesty remains, beyond the sphere of human contention.

The plain, that contains the village and the spa, is about five miles in length and of half that breadth. It is covered by uninclosed corn, and nearly surrounded by a vast amphitheatre of mountains. In front of the inn, at the distance of half a league, extend, along the opposite shore of the Rhine, the Seven Mountains, so long seen and admired, which here assume a new attitude. The three tallest points are now nearest to the eye, and the lower mountains are seen either in the perspective between them, or sinking, with less abrupt declivities, into the plains, on the north. The whole mass exhibits a grandeur of outline, such as the pencil only can describe; but fancy may paint the stupendous precipices of rock, that rise over the Rhine, the rich tuftings of wood, that emboss the cliffs or

lurk

lurk within the recesses, the spiry summits and the ruined castles, faintly discerned, that crown them. Yet the appearance of these mountains, though more grand, from Goodesberg, is less sublime than from Bonn; for the nearness, which increases their grandeur, diminishes their sublimity by removing the obscurity that had veiled them. To the south of this plain, the long perspective is crossed by further ranges of mountains, which open to glimpses of others still beyond; an endless succession of summits, that lead on the imagination to unknown vallies and regions of solitary obscurity.

Amidst so many attractions of nature, art cannot do much. The little, which it attempts, at Goodesberg, is the disposition of some walks from the houses to a spring, which is said to resemble that at Spa, and through the woods above it. Twice a week there are some musical performances and a ball

ball given by the Elector, who frequently appears, and with the ease and plainness of a private gentleman. At these entertainments the company, visiting the spring, are joined by neighbouring families, so as to be in number sixty, or a hundred. The balls, agreeably to the earliness of German hours, begin at six; and that, which we meant to see, was nearly concluded before our arrival. The company then retired to a public game, at which large sums of gold were risked, and a severe anxiety defied the influence of Mozart's music, that continued to be played by an excellent orchestra. The dresses of the company were in the English taste, and, as we were glad to believe, chiefly of English manufacture; the wearing of countenances by play appears to be also according to our manners; and the German ladies, with features scarcely less elegant, have complexions, perhaps, finer than are general in England.

Meditating

GERMANY.

Meditating censures against the Elector's policy, or carelessness, in this respect, we took advantage of the last gleams of evening, to ascend the slender and spiry mountain, which bears the name of the village, and appears ready to precipitate the ruins of its antient castle upon it. A steep road, winding among vineyards and dwarf wood, enters, at the summit of the mountain, the broken walls, which surround the antient citadel of the castle; an almost solid building, that has existed for more than five centuries. From the area of these ruins we saw the sun set over the whole line of plains, that extend to the westward of Cologne, whose spires were distinctly visible. Bonn, and the hill SANCTÆ CRUCIS, appeared at a league's distance, and the windings of the Rhine gleamed here and there amidst the rich scene, like distant lakes. It was a still and beautiful evening, in which no shade remained of the thunder clouds, that paffed in the day. To the weft, under the glow of fun-fet, the landfcape melted into the horizon in tints fo foft, fo clear, fo delicately rofeate as Claude only could have painted. Viewed, as we then faw it, beyond a deep and dark arch of the ruin, its effect was enchanting; it was to the eye, what the fineft ftrains of Paifiello are to the heart, or the poetry of Collins is to the fancy—all tender, fweet, elegant and glowing.

From the other fide of the hill the character of the view is entirely different, and, inftead of a long profpect over an open and level country, the little plain of Goodefberg appears repofing amidft wild and awful mountains. Thefe were now melancholy and filent; the laft rays were fading from their many points, and the obfcurity of twilight began to fpread over them. We feemed to have found the fpot, for which Collins wifhed:

" Now

" Now let me rove some wild and heathy
 scene,
Or find some ruin 'midst its dreary dells,
Whose walls more awful nod
By thy religious gleams."
                              ODE TO EVENING.

And this is a place almost as renowned in the history of the country, as it is worthy to exercise the powers of poetry and painting. The same Ernest, in the cause of whose sovereignty the massacre of Neuss was perpetrated, besieged here the same Gerard de Trusches, the Elector, who had embraced the Protestant religion, and for whom Neuss held out. The castle of Goodesberg was impregnable, except by famine, but was very liable to that from its insulated situation, and the ease, with which the whole base of the mountain could be surrounded. Gerard's defence was rendered the more obstinate by his belief, that nothing less than his life, and that of a

beautiful

beautiful woman, the marrying of whom had conſtituted one of the offences againſt his Chapter, would appeaſe his ferocious enemies. He was perſonally beloved by his garriſon, and they adhered to him with the affection of friends, as well as with the enthuſiaſm of ſoldiers. When, therefore, they perceived, that their ſurrender could not be much longer protracted, they reſolved to employ their remaining time and ſtrength in enabling him to ſeparate his fortunes from theirs. They laboured inceſſantly in forming a ſubterraneous paſſage, which ſhould open beyond the beſiegers' lines; and, though their diſtreſs became extreme before this was completed, they made no overtures for a ſurrender, till Gerard and his wife had eſcaped by it. The fugitives arrived ſafely in Holland, and the vengeance of their adverſaries was never gratified further than by hearing, many years after, that they died poor.

The fortress, rendered interesting by these traits of fidelity and misfortune, is not so far decayed, but that its remains exhibit much of its original form. It covered the whole summit of the hill, and was valuable as a residence, as well as a fortification. What seem to have been the walls of the great hall, in which probably the horn of two quarts was often emptied to welcome the guest, or reward the soldier, are still perfect enough to preserve the arches of its capacious windows, and the door-ways, that admitted its festive trains. The vast strength of the citadel has been unsubdued by war, or time. Though the battlements, that crown it, are broken, and of a gallery, that once encircled it half way from the ground, the corbells alone remain, the solid walls of the building itself are unimpaired. At the narrow door-way, by which only it could be entered, we measured their thickness, and found it to be more than ten feet, nearly half the diameter of its area. There has never been a fixed staircase, though these walls would so well have contained one; and the hole is still perfect in the floor above, through which the garrison ascended, and drew up their ladder after them. Behind the loop-holes, the wall has been hollowed, and would permit a soldier, half bent, to stand within them and use his bow. It was twilight without and night within the edifice; which fancy might have easily filled with the stern and silent forms of warriors, waiting for their prey, with the patience of safety and sure superiority.

We wandered long among these vestiges of ancient story, rendered still more interesting by the shadowy hour and the vesper bell of a chapel on a cliff below. The village, to which this belongs, straggles half way up the mountain, and there are several little shrines above it, which the cottagers,

on

on festivals, decorate with flowers. The Priest is the schoolmaster of the parish, and almost all the children, within several miles of the hill, walk to it, every day, to prayers and lessons. Whether it is from this care of their minds, or that they are under the authority of milder landlords than elsewhere, the manners of the inhabitants in this plain differ much from those, usual in Germany. Instead of an inveterate sullenness, approaching frequently to malignity, they shew a civility and gentleness in their intercourse with strangers, which leave the enjoyments derived from inanimate nature, unalloyed by the remembrances of human deformity, that mingle with them in other districts. Even the children's begging is in a manner, which shews a different character. They here kiss their little hands, and silently hold them out to you, almost as much in salute, as in entreaty; in many parts of Germany their manner is so offensive, not only for its intrusion, but as a symptom of their disposition, that nothing but the remembrance of the oppression, that produces it, can prevent you from denying the little they are compelled to require.

The music had not ceased, when we returned to the inn; and the mellowness of French horns, mingled with the tenderness of hautboys, gave a kind of enchantment to the scenery, which we continued to watch from our windows. The opposite mountains of the Rhine were gradually vanishing in twilight and then as gradually re-appearing, as the rising moon threw her light upon their broken surfaces. The perspective in the east received a silvery softness, which made its heights appear like shadowy illusions, while the nearer mountains were distinguished by their colouring, as much as by their forms. The broad Rhine, at their feet, rolled a stream of light for their boundary, on this side. But the
first

first exquisite tint of beauty soon began to fade; the mountains became misty underneath the moon, and, as she ascended, these mists thickened, till they veiled the landscape from our view.

The spring, which is supposed to have some medicinal qualities, is about a quarter of a mile from the rooms, in a woody valley, in which the Elector has laid out several roads and walks. It rises in a stone bason, to which the company, if they wish to drink it on the spot, descend by an handsome flight of steps. We were not told its qualities, but there is a ferrugineous tint upon all the stones, which it touches. The taste is slightly unpleasant.

The three superior points of the Seven Mountains, which contribute so much to the distinction of Goodesberg, are called Drakenfels, Wolkenbourg and Lowenbourg, and have each been crowned by its castle, of which two are still visible in ruins.

There

There is a story faintly recorded, concerning them. Three brothers, resolving to found three distinguished families, took the method, which was anciently in use for such a purpose, that of establishing themselves in fortresses, from whence they could issue out, and take what they wanted from their industrious neighbours. The pinnacles of Drakenfels, Wolkenbourg and Lowenbourg, which, with all assistance, cannot be ascended now, without the utmost fatigue, were inaccessible, when guarded by the castles, built by the three brothers. Their depredations, which they called successes in war, enriched their families, and placed them amongst the most distinguished in the Empire.

They had a sister, named Adelaide, famed to have been very beautiful; and, their parents being dead, the care of her had descended to them. Roland, a young knight, whose castle was on the opposite bank of the Rhine, became her suitor, and gained her affections. Whether the brothers had expected, by her means, to form a more splendid alliance, or that they remembered the ancient enmity between their family and that of Roland, they secretly resolved to deny the hand of Adelaide, but did not choose to provoke him by a direct refusal. They stipulated, that he should serve, a certain number of years, in the war of Palestine, and, on his return, should be permitted to renew his suit.

Roland took a reluctant farewell of Adelaide, and went to the war, where he was soon distinguished for an impetuous career. Adelaide remained in the castle of Drakenfels, waiting, in solitary fidelity, for his return. But the brothers had determined, that he should not return for her. They clothed one of their dependents in the disguise of a pilgrim, and introduced him into the castle, where he related that he was arrived

arrived from the holy wars, and had been defired by Roland in his lateſt moments to aſſure Adelaide of his having loved her till death.

The unhappy Adelaide believed the tale, and, from that time, devoted herſelf to the memory of Roland and to the nouriſhment of her ſorrow. She rejected all the ſuitors, introduced by her brothers, and accepted no ſociety, but that of ſome neighbouring nuns. At length, the gloom of a cloiſter became ſo neceſſary to the melancholy of her imagination, that ſhe reſolved to found a convent and take the veil; a deſign, which her brothers aſſiſted, with the view of placing her effectually beyond the reach of her lover. She choſe an iſland in the Rhine between her brother's caſtle and the ſeat of Roland, both of which ſhe could ſee from the windows of her convent; and here ſhe paſſed ſome years in the placid performance of her new duties.

At

GERMANY.

At length, Roland returned, and they both difcovered the cruel device, by which they had been feparated for ever. Adelaide remained in her convent, and foon after died; but Roland, emulating the fidelity of her retirement, built, at the extreme point of his domains towards the Rhine, a fmall caftle, that overlooked the ifland, where he wafted his days in melancholy regret, and in watching over the walls, that fhrouded his Adelaide.

This is the ftory, on which the wild and vivid imagination of Ariofto is faid to have founded his Orlando.

THE VALLEY OF ANDERNACH.

AFTER fpending part of two days at Goodefberg, we fet out, in a fultry afternoon, for the town of Andernach, diftant

tant about five-and-twenty Englifh miles. The road wound among corn-lands towards the Rhine, and approached almoſt as near to the Seven Mountains, as the river would permit. Oppofite to the laſt, and nearly the talleſt of thefe, called Drakenfels, the open plain terminates, and the narrower valley begins.

This mountain towers, the majeſtic fentinel of the river over which it afpires, in vaſt maſſes of rock, varied with rich tuftings of dwarf-wood, and bearing on its narrow peak the remains of a caſtle, whofe walls feem to rife in a line with the perpendicular precipice, on which they ſtand, and, when viewed from the oppofite bank, appear little more than a rugged cabin. The eye aches in attempting to fcale this rock; but the fublimity of its height and the grandeur of its intermingled cliffs and woods gratify the warmeſt wifh of fancy.

The road led us along the weſtern bank
of

of the Rhine among vineyards, and corn, and thick-trees, that allowed only tranfient catches of the water between their branches; but the gigantic form of Drakenfels was always feen, its fuperior features, perhaps, appearing more wild, from the partial concealment of its bafe, and affuming new attitudes as we paffed away from it. Lowenberg, whofe upper region only had been feen from Goodefberg, foon unfolded itfelf from behind Drakenfels, and difplayed all its pomp of wood, fweeping from the fpreading bafe in one uninterrupted line of grandeur to the fpiry top, on which one high tower of the caftle appears enthroned among the forefts. This is the loftieft of the Seven Mountains; and its dark fides, where no rock is vifible, form a fine contraft with the broken cliffs of Drakenfels. A multitude of fpiry fummits appeared beyond Lowenberg, feen and loft again, as the nearer rocks of the fhore opened to the diftance, distance, or re-united. About a mile further, lies the pleasant island, on which Adelaide raised her convent. As it was well endowed, it has been rebuilt, and is now a large and handsome quadrangle of white stone, surrounded with trees, and corn, and vineyards, and still allotted to the society, which she established. An abrupt, but not lofty rock, on the western shore of the Rhine, called Rolands Eck, or Roland's Corner, is the site of her lover's castle, of which one arch, picturesquely shadowed with wood, is all that remains of this monument to faithful love. The road winds beneath it, and nearly overhangs the narrow channel, that separates Adelaide's island from the shore. Concerning this rock there is an antient rhyme in the country, amounting to something like the following:

Was not Roland, the knight, a strange silly wight,
For the love of a nun, to live on this height?

After

After paffing the ifland, the valley contracts, and the river is foon fhut up between fruitful and abrupt hills, which rife immediately over it, on one fide, and a feries of rocky heights on the other. In the fmall fpace, left between thefe heights and the Rhine, the road is formed. For the greater part of the way, it has been hollowed in the folid rock, which afcends almoft perpendicularly above it, on one hand, and finks as abruptly below it, to the river, on the other; a work worthy of Roman perfeverance and defign, and well known to be a monument of both. It was made during the reign of Marcus Aurelius and Lucius Verus; and as the infcription, whofe antiquity has not been doubted, dates its completion in the year 162, it muft have been finifhed in one year, or little more, Marcus Aurelius having been raifed to the purple in 161. The Elector Palatine having repaired this road, which the Electors of Cologne had neglected, in 1768, has caufed his name to be joined with thofe of the Roman Emperors, in the following infcription upon an obelifk:

VIAM
SUB M.
AURELIO
ET L. VERO
I. M. P. P.
ANNO CHR.
CLXII
MUNITAM
CAROLUS
THEODORUS
ELECTOR PAL.
DUX BAV. JUL. CL. M.
REFECIT
ET AMPLIAVIT
AN. M.DCCLXVIII
CURANTE JO. LUD. COMITE
DE GOLDSTEIN
PRO PRINCIPE.

We did not fufficiently obferve the commencement and conclufion of this road, to be certain of its exact length; but it is probably

bably about twelve miles. The rock above is, for the moſt part, naked to the ſummit, where it is thinly covered with earth; but ſometimes it ſlopes ſo much as to permit patches of ſoil on its ſide, and theſe are carefully planted with vines. This ſhore of the Rhine may be ſaid to be bounded, for many miles, by an immenſe wall of rock, through which the openings into the country behind are few; and theſe breaks ſhew only deep glens, ſeen and loſt again ſo quickly, that a woody mountain, or a caſtle, or a convent, were the only objects we could aſcertain.

This rock lies in oblique *ſtrata*, and reſembles marble in its brown and reddiſh tints, marked with veins of deeper red; but we are unable to mention it under its proper and ſcientific denomination. The colouring of the cliffs is beautiful, when mingled with the verdure of ſhrubs, that ſometimes hang in rich drapery from their points, and with the moffes, and creeping vegetables of bright crimfon, yellow, and purple, that embofs their fractured fides.

The road, which the Elector mentions himfelf to have widened, is now and then very narrow, and approaches near enough to the river, over which it has no parapet, to make a traveller anxious for the fobriety and fkill of his poftillion. It is fometimes elevated forty feet above the level of the Rhine, and feldom lefs than thirty; an elevation from whence the water and its fcenery are viewed to great advantage; but to the variety and grandeur of thefe fhores, and the ever-changing form of the river, defcription cannot do juftice.

Sometimes, as we approached a rocky point, we feemed going to plunge into the expanfe of water beyond; when, turning the fharp angle of the promontory, the road fwept along an ample bay, where the rocks, receding, formed an amphitheatre, covered

covered with *ilex* and dwarf-wood, round a narrow, but cultivated level stripe; then, winding the furthest angle of this crescent, under huge cliffs, we saw the river beyond, shut in by the folding bases of more distant promontories, assume the form of a lake, amidst wild and romantic landscapes. Having doubled one of these capes, the prospect opened in long perspective, and the green waters of the Rhine appeared in all their majesty, flowing rapidly between ranges of marbled rocks, and a succession of woody steeps, and overlooked by a multitude of spiry summits, which distance had sweetly coloured with the blue and purple tints of air.

The retrospect of the river, too, was often enchanting, and the Seven Mountains long maintained their dignity in the scene, superior to many intervening heights; the dark summit of Lowenbourg, in particular, appeared,

appeared, for several leagues, overlooking the whole valley of the Rhine.

The eastern margin of the river sometimes exhibited as extensive a range of steep rocks as the western, and frequently the fitness of the salient angles on one side, to the recipient ones on the other, seemed to justify the speculation, that they had been divided by an earthquake, which let the river in between them. The general state of the eastern bank, though steep, is that of the thickest cultivation. The rock frequently peeps, in rugged projections, through the thin soil, which is scattered over its declivity, and every where appears at top; but the sides are covered with vines so abundantly, that the labour of cultivating them, and of expressing the wine, supports a village at least at every half mile. The green rows are led up the steeps to an height, which cannot be ascended without

the

the help of steps cut in the rock: the soil itself is there supported by walls of loose stones, or it would fall either by its own weight, or with the first pressure of rain; and sometimes even this scanty mould appears to have been placed there by art, being in such small patches, that, perhaps, only twenty vines can be planted in each. But such excessive labour has been necessary only towards the summits, for, lower down, the soil is sufficiently deep to support the most luxuriant vegetation.

It might be supposed from so much produce and exertion, that this bank of the Rhine is the residence of an opulent, or, at least, a well-conditioned peasantry, and that the villages, of which seven or eight are frequently in sight at once, are as superior to the neighbouring towns by the state of their inhabitants, as they are by their picturesque situation. On the contrary, the inhabitants of the wine country are said to be amongst the poorest in Germany. The value of every hill is exactly watched by the landlords, so that the tenants are very seldom benefited by any improvement of its produce. If the rent is paid in money, it leaves only so much in the hands of the farmer as will enable him to live, and pay his workmen; while the attention of a great number of stewards is supposed to supply what might be expected from his attention, had he a common interest with his landlord in the welfare of the estate. But the rent is frequently paid in kind, amounting to a settled proportion of the produce; and this proportion is so fixed, that, though the farmer is immoderately distressed by a bad vintage, the best will not afford him any means of approaching to independence. In other countries it might be asked, " But, though we can suppose the ingenuity of the landlord to be greater than that of the tenant, at the commencement of a bargain, a bargain, how happens it, that, since the result must be felt, the tenant will remain under his burthens, or can be succeeded by any other, on such terms?" Here, however, these questions are not applicable; they presume a choice of situations, which the country does not afford. The severity of the agricultural system continues itself by continuing the poverty, upon which it acts; and those who would escape from it find few manufactures and little trade to employ them, had they the capital and the education necessary for either. The choice of such persons is between the being a master of day-labourers for their landlord, or a labourer under other masters.

Many of these estates belong immediately to Princes, or Chapters, whose stewards superintend the cultivation, and are themselves instead of the farmers, so that all other persons employed in such vineyards are ordinary servants. By one or other of these means

means it happens, that the bounteousness of nature to the country is very little felt by the body of the inhabitants. The payment of rents in kind is usual, wherever the vineyards are most celebrated; and, at such places, there is this sure proof of the wretchedness of the inhabitants, that, in a month after the wine is made, you cannot obtain one bottle of the true produce, except by favour of the proprietors, or their stewards. How much is the delight of looking upon plenteousness lessened by the belief, that it supplies the means of excess to a few, but denies those of competence to many!

Between this pass of cultivated steeps on one side of the river, and of romantic rocks on the other, the road continues for several miles. Being thus commanded on both sides, it must be one of the most difficult passages in Europe to an enemy, if resolutely defended. The Rhine, pent between these impenetrable boundaries, is considerably

bly narrower here than in other parts of the valley, and fo rapid, that a loaded veffel can feldom be drawn fafter than at the rate of fix Englifh miles a day, againft the ftream. The paffage down the river from Mentz to Cologne may be eafily performed in two days; that from Cologne to Mentz requires a fortnight.

The view along this pafs, though bounded, is various and changeful. Villages, vineyards and rocks alternately ornament the borders of the river, and every fifty yards enable the eye to double fome maffy projection that concealed the fruitful bay behind. An object at the end of the pafs is prefented fingly to the fight as through an inverted telefcope. The furface of the water, or the whole ftillnefs of the fcene, was very feldom interrupted by the paffing of a boat; carriages were ftill fewer; and, indeed, throughout Germany, you will not meet more than one in twenty miles.

Travelling is considered by the natives, who know the fatigue of going in carriages nearly without springs, and stopping at inns where there is little of either accommodation or civility, as productive of no pleasure; and they have seldom curiosity or business enough to recompense for its inconveniencies.

We passed through two or three small towns, whose ruined gates and walls told of their antiquity, and that they had once been held of some consequence in the defence of the valley. Their present desolation formed a melancholy contrast with the cheerful cultivation around them. These, however, with every village in our way, were decorated with green boughs, planted before the door of each cottage, for it was a day of festival. The little chapels at the roadside, and the image, which, every now and then, appeared under a spreading tree, were adorned with wreaths of fresh flowers;

and

GERMANY. 269

and though one might smile at the emblems of superstition, it was impossible not to reverence the sentiment of pious affection, which had adjusted these simple ornaments.

About half-way to Andernach, the western rocks suddenly recede from the river, and, rising to greater height, form a grand sweep round a plain cultivated with orchards, garden-fields, corn and vineyards. The valley here spreads to a breadth of nearly a mile and an half, and exhibits grandeur, beauty and barren sublimity, united in a singular manner. The abrupt steeps, that rise over this plain, are entirely covered with wood, except that here and there the ravage of a winter torrent appeared, which could sometimes be traced from the very summit of the acclivity to the base. Near the centre, this noble amphitheatre opens to a glen, that shews only wooded mountains, point above point, in long perspective;

spective; such sylvan pomp we had seldom seen! But though the tuftings of the nearer woods were beautifully luxuriant, there seemed to be few timber trees amongst them. The opposite shore exhibited only a range of rocks, variegated like marble, of which purple was the predominating tint, and uniformly disposed in vast, oblique strata. But even here, little green patches of vines peeped among the cliffs, and were led up crevices where it seemed as if no human foot could rest. Along the base of this tremendous wall, and on the points above, villages, with each its tall, grey steeple, were thickly strewn, thus mingling in striking contrast the cheerfulness of populous inhabitation with the horrors of untamed nature. A few monasteries, resembling castles in their extent, and known from such only by their spires, were distinguishable; and, in the widening perspective of the Rhine, an old castle itself, now and then,

then, appeared on the summit of a mountain somewhat remote from the shore; an object rendered sweetly picturesque, as the sun's rays lighted up its towers and fortified terraces, while the shrubby steeps below were in shade.

We saw this landscape under the happiest circumstances of season and weather; the woods and plants were in their midsummer bloom, and the mellow light of evening heightened the richness of their hues, and gave exquisite effect to one half of the amphitheatre we were passing, while the other half was in shadow. The air was scented by bean-blossoms, and by lime-trees then in flower, that bordered the road. If this plain had mingled pasture with its groves, it would have been truly Arcadian; but neither here, nor through the whole of this delightful valley, did we see a single pasture or meadow, except now and then in

an

an island on the Rhine; deficiencies which are here supplied, to the lover of landscape, by the verdure of the woods and vines. In other parts of Germany they are more to be regretted, where, frequently, only corn and rock colour the land.

Fatigued at length by such prodigality of beauty, we were glad to be shrouded awhile from the view of it, among close boughs, and to see only the wide rivulets, with their rustic bridges of faggots and earth, that, descending from among the mountains, frequently crossed our way; or the simple peasant-girl, leading her cows to feed on the narrow stripe of grass that margined the road. The little bells, that jingled at their necks, would not suffer them to stray beyond her hearing. If we had not long since dismissed our surprise at the scarcity and bad quality of cheese and butter in Germany, we should have done so now, on perceiving

perceiving this scanty method of pasturing the cattle, which future observation convinced us was the frequent practice.

About sun-set we reached the little village of Namedy, seated near the foot of a rock, round which the Rhine makes a sudden sweep, and, contracted by the bold precipices of Hammerstein on the opposite shore, its green current passes with astonishing rapidity and sounding strength. These circumstances of scenery, with the tall masts of vessels lying below the shrubby bank, on which the village stands, and seeming to heighten by comparison the stupendous rocks, that rose around them; the moving figures of boatmen and horses employed in towing a barge against the stream, in the bay beyond; and a group of peasants on the high quay, in the fore ground, watching their progress; the ancient castle of Hammerstein overlooking the whole—these were a combination of images, that formed

T   one

one of the moſt intereſting pictures we had ſeen.

The valley again expanding, the walls and turrets of Andernach, with its Roman tower riſing independently at the foot of a mountain, and the ruins of its caſtle above, appeared athwart the perſpective of the river, terminating the paſs; for there the rocky boundary opened to plains and remote mountains. The light vapour, that roſe from the water, and was tinged by the ſetting rays, ſpread a purple haze over the town and the cliffs, which, at this diſtance, appeared to impend over it; colouring extremely beautiful, contraſted as it was by the clearer and deeper tints of rocks, wood and water nearer to the eye.

As we approached Andernach, its ſituation ſeemed to be perpetually changing, with the winding bank. Now it appeared ſeated on a low peninſula, that nearly croſſed the Rhine, overhung by romantic rocks;

rocks; but this vifion vanifhed as we advanced, and we perceived the town lying along a curving fhore, near the foot of the cliffs, which were finely fringed with wood, and at the entrance of extenfive plains. Its towers feen afar, would be figns of a confiderable place, to thofe who had not before been wearied of fuch fymptoms by the towers of Neufs, and other German towns. From a wooded precipice over the river we had foon after a fine retrofpective glimpfe of the valley, its fantaftic fhores, and long mountainous diftance, over which evening had drawn her fweeteft colouring. As we purfued the pafs, the heights on either hand gradually foftened; the country beyond fhewed remote mountains lefs wild and afpiring than thofe we had left, and the blooming tint, which had invefted the diftance, deepened to a dufky purple, and then vanifhed in the gloom of twilight. The progreffive influence of the hour upon the landscape was interesting; and the shade of evening, under which we entered Andernach, harmonized with the desolation and silence of its old walls and the broken ground around them. We passed a drawbridge and a ruinous gateway, and were sufficiently fatigued to be somewhat anxious as to our accommodation. The English habit of considering, towards the end of the day's journey, that you are not far from the cheerful reception, the ready attendance, and the conveniences of a substantial inn, will soon be lost in Germany. There, instead of being in good spirits, during the last stage, from such a prospect, you have to consider, whether you shall find a room, not absolutely disgusting, or a house with any eatable provision, or a landlady, who will give it you, before the delay and the fatigue of an hundred requests have rendered you almost incapable of receiving it. When your carriage stops at the inn, you will

will perhaps perceive, inftead of the alacrity of an Englifh waiter, or the civility of an Englifh landlord, a huge figure, wrapt in a great coat, with a red worfted cap on his head, and a pipe in his mouth, ftalking before the door. This is the landlord. He makes no alteration in his pace on perceiving you, or, if he ftops, it is to eye you with curiofity ; he feldom fpeaks, never bows, or affifts you to alight; and perhaps ftands furrounded by a troop of flovenly girls, his daughters, whom the found of wheels has brought to the door, and who, as they lean indolently againft it, gaze at you with rude curiofity and furprife.

The drivers in Germany are all bribed by the innkeepers, and, either by affecting to mifunderftand you, or otherwife, will conftantly ftop at the door, where they are beft paid. That this money comes out of your pocket the next morning is not the grievance; the evil is, that the worft inns give

give them the moft, and a traveller, unlefs he exactly remembers his directions, is liable to be lodged in all the vileft rooms of a country, where the beft hotels have no lodging fo clean and no larder fo wholefomely filled as thofe of every half-way houfe between London and Canterbury. When you are within the inn, the landlord, who is eager to keep, though not to accommodate you, will affirm, that his is the inn you afk for, or that the other fign is not in the place; and, as you foon learn to believe any thing of the wretchednefs of the country, you are unwilling to give up one lodging, left you fhould not find another.

Our driver, after paffing a defolate, half filled place, into which the gate of Andernach opened, entered a narrow paffage, which afterwards appeared to be one of the chief ftreets of the place. Here he found a miferable inn, and declared that there was no other; but, as we had feen one

one of a much better appearance, we were at length brought to that, and, though with some delay, were not ill accommodated, for the night.

Andernach is an antient town, and it is believed, that a tower, which ſtands alone, at one end of the walls, was built by Druſus, of whom there are many traces in walls and caſtles, intended to defend the colonies, on this ſide of the Rhine, againſt the Germans, on the other. The fortifications can now be of little other uſe than to authoriſe the toll, which travellers pay, for entering a walled town; a tax, on account of which many of the walls are ſupported, though it is pretended, that the tax is to ſupport the walls. By their means alſo, the Elector of Cologne collects here the laſt of four payments, which he demands for the privilege of paſſing the Rhine from Urdingen to Andernach; and this is the moſt Southern frontier town of his dominions on the western side of the Rhine, which soon after join those of the Elector of Treves. Their length from hence to Rheinberg is not less than ninety miles; the breadth probably never more than twenty.

There is some trade, at Andernach, in tiles, timber, and mill-stones, but the heaps of these commodities upon the beach are the only visible symptoms of the traffick; for you will not see one person in the place moving as if he had business to attract him, or one shop of a better appearance, than an English huckster's, or one man in the dress of a creditable trader, or one house, which can be supposed to belong to persons in easy circumstances. The port contains, perhaps, half a dozen vessels, clinker built, in shape between a barge and a sloop; on the quay, you may see two or three fellows, harnessing half a dozen horses to a tow line, while twenty more watch their lingering manœuvres,

manœuvres, and this may probably be the morning's bufinefs of the town. Thofe, who are concerned in it, fay that they are engaged in *commerce*.

This, or fomething like it, is the condition, as to trade, of all the towns we faw in Germany, one or two excepted. They are fo far from having well filled, or fpacious repofitories, that you can fcarcely tell at what houfes there are any, till you are led within the door; you may then wait long after you are heard, or feen, before the owner, if he has any other engagement, thinks it neceffary to approach you : if he has what you afk for, which he probably has not, unlefs it is fomething very ordinary, he tells the price and takes it, with as much fullennefs, as if you were forcing the goods from him : if he has not, and can fhew you only fomething very different, he then confiders your enquiry as an intrufion, and appears to think himfelf injured by

having

having had the trouble to answer you. What seems unaccountable in the manners of a German trader, is, that, though he is so careless in attending you, he looks as much distressed, as vexed, if you do not leave some money with him; but he probably knows, that you can be supplied no where else in the town, and, therefore, will not deny himself the indulgence of his temper. Even when you are satisfied, his manner is so ill, that he appears to consider you his dependent, by wanting something which he can refuse. After perceiving, that this is nearly general, the pain of making continual discoveries of idleness and malignity becomes so much greater than the inconvenience of wanting any thing short of necessaries, that you decline going into shops, and wait for some easier opportunities of supplying whatever you may lose upon the road.

COBLENTZ.

COBLENTZ.

IT is one post from Andernach hi‑ ther, over a road, as good as any in Eng‑ land. Beyond the dominions of the Elec‑ tor of Cologne, the face of the country, on this side of the Rhine, entirely changes its character. The rocks cease, at Andernach, and a rich plain commences, along which the road is led, at a greater distance from the Rhine, through corn lands and unin‑ closed orchards. About a mile from An‑ dernach, on the other side of the river, the white town of Neuwiedt, the capital of a small Protestant principality, is seen; and the general report, that it is one of the most commercial places, on the Rhine, appeared to be true from the cheerful neatness of the principal street, which faces towards the water. There were also about twenty small

vessels,

veſſels, lying before it, and the quay ſeemed to be wide enough to ſerve as a ſpacious terrace to the houſes. The Prince's palace, an extenſive ſtone building, with a lofty orangery along the ſhore, is at the end of this ſtreet, which, as well as the greateſt part of the town, was built, or improved under the auſpices of his father; a wiſe prince, diſtinguiſhed by having negotiated, in 1735, a peace between the Empire and France, when the continuance of the war had ſeemed to be inevitable. The ſame benevolence led him to a voluntary ſurrender of many oppreſſive privileges over his ſubjects, as well as to the moſt careful protection of commerce and manufactures. Accordingly, the town of Neuwiedt has been continually increaſing in proſperity and ſize, for the laſt fifty years, and the inhabitants of the whole principality are ſaid to be as much more qualified in their characters as they are happier in their conditions

tions than thofe of the neighbouring ftates. But then there is the *wretchednefs* of a deficiency of game in the country, for the late Prince was guilty of fuch an innovation as to mitigate the feverity of the laws refpecting it.

The foreft hills, that rife behind Neuwiedt and over the rocky margin of the river, extend themfelves towards the more rugged mountains of Wetteravia, which are feen, a fhapelefs multitude, in the eaft.

The river is foon after loft to the view between high, fedgy banks; but, near Coblentz, the broad bay, which it makes in conjunction with the Mofelle, is feen expanding between the walls of the city and the huge pyramidal precipice, on which ftands the fortrefs of Ehrenbreitftein, or rather which is itfelf formed into that fortrefs. The Mofelle is here a noble river, by which the ftreams of a thoufand hills, covered with vines, pour themfelves into the Rhine.

The

The antient stone bridge over it leads to the northern gate of Coblentz, and the entrance into the city is ornamented by several large chateau-like mansions, erected to command a view of the two rivers. A narrow street of high, but antient houses then commences, and runs through the place. Those, which branch from it, extend, on each side, towards the walls, immediately within which there are others, that nearly follow their course and encompass the city. Being built between two rivers, its form is triangular, and only one side is entirely open to the land; a situation so convenient both for the purposes of commerce and war, that it could not be overlooked by the Romans, and was not much neglected by the moderns, till the industry of maritime countries and the complicated constitution of the Empire reduced Germany in the scale of nations. This was accordingly the station of the first legion, and the union of the two rivers gave

it

it a name; *Confluentia*. At the commencement of the modern divifion of nations, the fucceffors of Charlemagne frequently refided here, for the convenience of an intercourfe between the other parts of the Empire and France; but, in the eleventh century, the whole territory of Treves regained the diftinction, as a feparate country, which the Romans had given it, by calling the inhabitants *Treveri*.

Coblentz is a city of many fpires, and has eftablifhments of chapters and monafteries, which make the great pride of German capitals; and are fometimes the chief objects, that could diftinguifh them from the neglected villages of other countries. The ftreets are not all narrow, but few of them are ftraight; and the fame pavement ferves for the horfes of the Elector and the feet of his fubjects. The port, or beach, has the appearance of fomething more bufinefs than that of Andernach, being the refort of paffage-

sage-veffels between Mentz and Cologne;
but the broad quay, which has been raifed
above it, is chiefly useful as a promenade
to the vifitors of a clofe and gloomy town.
Beyond the terrace ftands the Elector's palace, an elegant and fpacious ftone edifice,
built to the height of three ftories, and in-
clofing a court, which is large enough to be
light as well as magnificent. The front towards the Rhine is fimple, yet grand, the
few ornaments being fo well proportioned
to its fize, as neither to debafe it by minute-
nefs, nor encumber it by vaftnefs. An en-
tablature, difplaying fome allegorical figures
in bas relief, is fupported by fix Doric columns, which contribute much to the majeftic fimplicity of the edifice. The palace
was built, about ten years fince, by the
reigning Elector, who mentions, in an infcription, his attention to the architectural
art; and a fountain, between the building
and the town, is infcribed with a few words,
which

which seem to acknowledge his subjects as beings of the same species with himself; CLEMENS WINCESLAUS VICINIS SUIS.

But the most striking parts of the view from this quay are the rock and fortress of Ehrenbreitstein, that present themselves immediately before it, on the other side of the river; notwithstanding the breadth of which they appear to rise almost perpendicularly over Coblentz. At the base of the rock stands a large building, formerly the palace of the Electors, who chose to reside under the immediate protection of the fortress, rather than in the midst of their capital. Adjoining it is the village of Ehrenbreitstein, between which and Coblentz a flying bridge is continually passing, and, with its train of subordinate boats, forms a very picturesque object from the quay. The fortress itself consists of several tier of low walls, built wherever there was a projection in the rock capable of supporting them, or wherever

wherever the rock could be hewn so as to afford room for cannon and soldiers. The stone, taken out of the mass, served for the formation of the walls, which, in some places, can scarcely be distinguished from the living rock. Above these tier, which are divided into several small parts, according to the conveniences afforded by the cliff, is built the castle, or citadel, covering its summit, and surrounded by walls more regularly continued, as well as higher. Small towers, somewhat in the antient form, defend the castle, which would be of little value, except for its height, and for the gradations of batteries between it and the river. Thus protected, it seems impregnable on that side, and is said to be not much weaker on the other; so that the garrison, if they should be willing to fire upon Coblentz, might make it impossible for an enemy to remain within it, except under the cover of very high entrenchments.

ments. This is the real defence of the city, for its walls would prefently fall before heavy artillery; and this, it is believed, might be preferved as long as the garrifon could be fupplied with ftores.

We croffed the river from the quay to the fortrefs, by means of the very fimple invention, a flying bridge. That, by which part of the paffage of the Waal is made at Nimeguen, has been already mentioned; this is upon the fame principle, but on a much larger fcale. After the barges, upon which the platform is laid, are clear of the bank, the whole paffage is effected with no other labour than that of the rudder. A ftrong cable, which is faftened to an anchor at each fide of the river, is fupported acrofs it by a feries of fmall boats; the bridge has two low mafts, one on each barge, and thefe are connected at the top by a beam, over which the cable is paffed, being confined fo as that it cannot flip beyond them.

When the bridge is launched, the rapidity of the current forces it down the Rhine as far as the cable will permit: having reached that point, the force, received from the current, gives it the only direction of which it is capable, that acrofs the river, with the cable which holds it. The fteerfman manages two rudders, by which he affifts in giving it this direction. The voyage requires nine or ten minutes, and the bridge is continually paffing. The toll, which, for a foot paffenger, is fomething lefs than a penny, is paid, for the benefit of the Elector, at an office, on the bank, and a fentinel always accompanies the bridge, to fupport his government, during the voyage.

The old palace of Ehrenbreitftein, deferted becaufe of its dampnefs, and from the fear of its being overwhelmed by the rock, that fometimes fcatters its fragments upon it, is now ufed as a barrack and hofpital

pital for foldiers. It is a large building, even more pleafantly fituated than the new one, being oppofite to the entrance of the Mofelle into the Rhine; and its ftructure, which has been once magnificent, denotes fcarcely any other decay, than all buildings will fhew, after a few years' neglect. The rock has allowed little room for a garden, but there are fome ridiculous ornaments upon a very narrow ftrip of ground, which was probably intended for one.

The only entrance into the fortrefs, on this fide, is by a road, cut in the folid rock, under four gateways. It is fo fteep, that we were compelled to decline the honour of admiffion, but afcended it far enough to judge of the view, commanded from the fummit, and to be behind the batteries, of which fome were mounted with large brafs cannon. Coblentz lies beneath it, as open to infpection as a model upon a table. The fweeps of the Rhine and the meanders of the Mofelle, the one binding the plain, the other interfecting it, lead the eye towards diftant hills, that encircle the capacious level. The quay of the city, with the palace and the moving bridge, form an interefting picture immediately below, and we were unwilling to leave the rock for the dull and clofe ftreets of Coblentz. On our return, the extreme nakednefs of the new palace, which is not fheltered by trees, on any fide, withdrew our attention from the motley group of paffengers, mingled with hay carts and other carriages, on the flying bridge.

The long refidence of the emigrant princes and nobleffe of France in this city is to be accounted for not by its general accommodations, or gaieties, of which it is nearly as deficient as the others of Germany; but firft by the great hofpitality of the Elector towards them, and then by the convenience of its fituation for receiving intelligence

telligence from France, and for communicating with other countries. The Elector held frequent levies for the French nobility, and continued for them part of the splendour which they had enjoyed in their own country. The readiness for lending money upon property, or employments in France, was also so great, that those, who had not brought cash with them, were immediately supplied, and those, who had, were encouraged to continue their usual expences. We know it from some of the best possible authority, that, at the commencement of the march towards Longwy, money, at four per cent. was even pressed upon many, and that large sums were refused.

Here, and in the neighbourhood, between sixty and seventy squadrons of cavalry, consisting chiefly of those who had formerly enjoyed military, or other rank, were formed; each person being mounted and equipped chiefly at his own expence. We heard

heard several anecdotes of the confidence, entertained in this army, of a speedy arrival in Paris; but, as the persons, to whom they relate, are now under the pressure of misfortune, there would be as little pleasure as propriety in repeating them.

At Coblentz, we quitted, for a time, the left bank of the Rhine, in order to take the watering place of Selters, in our way to Mentz. Having crossed the river and ascended a steep road, near the fortress, we had fine glimpses of its walls, bastions and out-towers, and the heathy knolls, around them, with catches of distant country. The way continued to lie through the dominions of the Elector of Treves, which are here so distinguished for their wretchedness as to be named the *Siberia of Germany!* It is paved, and called a *chauffée*; but those, who have not experienced its ruggedness, can have no idea of it, except by supposing the pavement of a street torn up by a plough, and then

then suffered to fix itself, as it had fallen. Always steep, either in ascent or descent, it is not only the roughness, that prevents your exceeding the usual post-pace of three English miles an hour. Sometimes it runs along edges of mountains, that might almost be called precipices, and commands short views of other mountains and of vallies entirely covered with thick, but not lofty forests; sometimes it buries itself in the depths of such forests and glens; sometimes the turrets of an old chateau peep above these, but rather confirm than contradict the notion of their desolateness, having been evidently built for the purposes of the chace; and sometimes a mud village surprises you with a few inhabitants, emblems of the misery and savageness of the country.

These are the mountains of Wetteravia, the boundaries of many a former and far-seen prospect, then picturesque, sublime, or graceful, but now desolate, shaggy, and almost

most hideous; as in life, that, which is so grand as to charm at a distance, is often found to be forlorn, disgustful and comfortless by those, who approach it.

MONTABAUR.

Six hours after leaving Coblentz, we reached Montabaur, the first post-town on the road, and distant about eighteen miles. An ancient chateau, not strong enough to be a castle, nor light enough to be a good house, commands the town, and is probably the residence of the lord. The walls and gates shew the antiquity of Montabaur, but the ruggedness of its site should seem to prove, that there was no other place in the neighbourhood, on which a town could be built. Though it is situated in a valley, as to the nearer mountains, it is constructed

chiefly

chiefly on two sides of a narrow rock, the abrupt summit of which is in the centre of this very little place.

The appearance of Montabaur is adequate in gloominess to that of several before seen; but it would be endless to repeat, as often as they should be true, the descriptions of the squalidness and decay, that characterise German towns; nor should we have noticed these so often, if the negligence of others, in this respect, had not left us to form deceitful expectations, suitable to the supposed importance of several very conspicuous, but really very wretched cities.

LIMBOURG.

OVER a succession of forest mountains, similar to those just passed, we came, in the afternoon, to Limbourg, another post town,

town, or, perhaps, city, and another collection of houses, like tombs, or forsaken hospitals. At an inn, called the Three Kings, we saw first the sullenness and then the ferocious malignity of a German landlord and his wife, exemplified much more fully than had before occurred. When we afterwards expressed our surprise, that the magistrates should permit persons of such conduct to keep an inn, especially where there was only one, we learned, that this fellow was himself the chief magistrate, or burgomaster of the place; and his authority appeared in the fearfulness of his neighbours to afford any sort of refreshment to those, who had left his inn. One of the Elector's ministers, with whom we had the pleasure to be acquainted, informed us, that he knew this man, and that he must have been intoxicated, for that, though civil when sober, he was madly turbulent and abusive, if otherwise. It appeared, therefore, that a

person

person was permitted to be a magistrate, who, to the knowledge of government, was exposed by his situation to be intoxicated, and was outrageous, whenever he was so. So little is the order of society estimated here, when it is not connected with the order of politics.

Near Limbourg, the forest scenery, which had shut up the view, during the day, disappeared, and the country lost, at least, an uniformity of savageness. The hills continue, but they are partly cultivated. At a small distance from the town, a steep ascent leads to a plain, on which a battle was fought, during the short stay of the French in this district, in the campaign of 1792. Four thousand French were advancing towards Limbourg; a small Prussian corps drew up to oppose them, and the engagement, though short, was vivid, for the Prussians did not perceive the superiority of the French in numbers, till the latter began to spread upon the plain, for the purpose of surrounding them. Being then compelled to retreat, they left several of the Elector's towns open to contribution, from which five-and-twenty thousand florins were demanded, but the remonstrances of the magistrates reduced this sum to 8000 florins, or about 700 l. The French then entered Limbourg, and extended themselves over the neighbouring country. At Weilbourg, the residence of a Prince of the House of Nassau, they required 300,000 florins, or 25,000 l. which the Prince neither had, nor could collect, in two days, through his whole country. All his plate, horses, coaches, arms and six pieces of cannon, were brought together, for the purpose of removal; but afterwards two individuals were accepted as hostages, instead of the Prince himself, who had been at first demanded. The action near Limbourg took place on the 9th of November, and, before the

the conclusion of the month, the French had fallen back to Franckfort, upon the re-approach of the Prussian and Austrian troops.

SELTERS.

WE had a curiosity to see this place, which, under the name of Seltzer, is so celebrated throughout Europe, for its medicinal water. Though it is rather in the high road to Franckfort than to Mentz, there seemed no probability of inconvenience in making this short departure from our route, when it was to be joined again from a place of such public access as Selters appeared likely to be found.

About seven miles from Limbourg, a descent commences, at the bottom of which stands this village. What a reproof to the expectations of comfort, or convenience in Germany! Selters, a spot, to which a valetudinarian might be directed, with the prospect of his finding not only abundant accommodation, but many luxuries, Selters is literally and positively nothing more than an assemblage of miserable cottages, with one inn and two houses for officers of the Elector, stuck in a dirty pass, which more resembles a ditch than a road. The village may be said to be near half a mile long, because the huts, being mostly separated from each other, continue as far; and this length would increase its inconvenience to invalids, if such should ever stay there longer than to see it, for there is nothing like a swept path-way, and the road, in which they must walk, is probably always deeply covered with mud, being so when we were there in the beginning of July. There was then, however, not one stranger, besides ourselves, in the place, and

we

we found, that very rarely any aggravate the miseries of sickness by a stay at Selters.

The only lodgings to be had are at the inn, and fortunately for travellers this is not such as might be expected from the appearance of the village. Finding there the novelty of an obliging host and hostess, we were very well contented to have reached it, at night, though we were to stay there also the next day, being Sunday. The rooms are as good as those in the inns of German cities, and three, which are called Court Chambers, having been used by the Elector and lately by the King of Prussia, are better. These are as open as the others to strangers.

The spring is at the foot of one of several hills, which immediately surround the village, and is separated from the road by a small court yard. An oaken covering, at the height of ten or twelve feet, prevents rain from falling into the wooden bason,

X in

in which the stream rises; and two or three of the Elector's guards watch over it, that no considerable quantity may be taken, without payment of the duty, which forms a large part of his income. Many thousands of stone bottles are piled round this court, and, for the reputation of the spring, care is taken to fill them as immediately as possible, before their removal for exportation.

The policy of keeping this income intire is said to be a motive for neglecting the condition of the village. A duty could not well be demanded of those, who should drink at the spring, but is easily collected before the water is bottled for removal; it is, therefore, not wished, that there should be many visitors, at Selters. We did not hear this reason upon the spot, but it is difficult otherwise to account for a negligence, which prevents the inhabitants of the neighbouring country from being enriched

riched at the expence of wanderers from others.

Nor is it only a duty, but the whole profit of the traffick, till the water leaves the place, which rewards the care of the Elector. His office for the fale of it is eftablished here, and his agents alone tranfmit it into foreign countries. The bufinefs is fufficient to employ feveral clerks, and the number of bottles annually filled is fo immenfe, that, having omitted to write it down, we will not venture to mention it from memory. The water is brought to table conftantly and at an eafy price in all the towns near the Rhine. Mixed with Rhenifh wine and fugar it forms a delightful, but not always a fafe beverage, in hot weather. The acid of the wine, expelling the fixed air of other ingredients, occafions an effervefcence, like that of Champagne, but the liquor has not a fourth part of the obnoxious strength of the latter. The danger of drinking it is, that the acid may be too powerful for some constitutions.

After being surprised by the desolateness of the village, we were not less so to find amongst its few inhabitants one, whose manners and information, so far from bearing the character of the dreariness around him, were worthy of the best society in the most intelligent cities. This was the Commissary and Privy Counsellor of the Elector for the district, who, having heard, that there were some English visitors at the well, very frankly introduced himself to us by his civilities, and favoured us with his company in the afternoon. He had been in England, with many valuable introductions, and had formed from the talents and accomplishments of a distinguished Marquis an high opinion of the national character; a circumstance, which probably united with

his

his natural difpofition, in inducing him to emulate towards us the general politenefs of that truly honourable perfon.

When we enquired how the journey of the next day was to be performed, it appeared, that no other carriage could be hired in the place than a fort of one-horfe chair, which would take us to the next poft town, from whence we might proceed with the ufual chaifes. The driver walked at the fide of this uncouth carriage, which had fhafts and wheels ftrong enough for a waggon; and, either by the miftake or intention of his mafter in directing him, we were led, not to the poft town, for a chaife, if it could be had, but entirely through a foreft country to Mentz, by roads made only for the woodcutters, and, as it afterwards proved, known to few others, except to our ingenious voiturier. We did not pafs a town, or village, at which it was poffible to change the carriage, and had, therefore, no other

other alternative, when the mistake was discovered, than to return to Selters, or to proceed to Mentz, in this inconvenient and ludicrous vehicle. We chose to proceed, and had some reward for fatigue, by passing nearly an whole day under the shade of deep and delightful forests, little tamed by the hand of man, and appearing to acknowledge only " the season's difference."

Between Selters and these forests, the country is well cultivated, and frequently laid out in garden-fields, in which there was the first appearance of cheerful labour we had seen in Germany. After passing a small town, on the summit of a hill to the left, still surrounded by its antient fortifications, we entered a large plain, skirted, on one side, by villages; another town, at the end of which, was almost the last sign of an inhabited country, that appeared for several hours. The forest then commenced, and, with the exception of one hamlet, enveloped

veloped near the middle, we saw nothing but lofty oaks, elms and chesnuts, till we emerged from it in the afternoon, and came to a town of the Landgrave of Hesse Darmstadt. Roebucks are said to be numerous, and wild boars not very scarce, in this forest; but we saw none either here, or in those near Limbourg, which are much inferior to this in beauty. Upon the whole, it was a scene of perfect novelty; without which it now seems that we should have wanted many ideas of sylvan life and much of the delight, excited by Shakespeare's exquisite description of it.

The country afterwards opens towards

MENTZ,

Which stands in a spacious plain, on the opposite edge of the Rhine, and is visible, at a considerable distance, with its massy towers and numerous spires. Within two or three miles of the city, the symptoms of ruin, occasioned by the siege in 1793, began to appear. A village, on the left, had scarcely one house entire; and the tower of the church was a mere wreck, blackened by flames, and with large chasms, that admitted the light. The road did not pass nearer to it than two miles, but the broken walls and roofs were distinguishable even at that distance, and sometimes a part, which had been repaired, contrasted its colour with the black and smoky hues of the remainder. This was the village of Kostheim, so often contended for in the course of the siege, being on the opposite bank of the Rhine to the city, and capable of obstructing the intercourse with it by water.

The country on the eastern side of the river was otherwise but little damaged, if we except the destruction of numerous orchards; for the allies were not strong enough

enough to befiege the city on all fides at once, and contented themfelves with occupying fome pofts in this quarter, capable of holding the garrifon of Caffel in awe.

This Caffel is a fmall village exactly oppofite to Mentz, and communicating with it by a bridge of boats. It was unfortified before the invafion of the French; but thefe had no fooner entered the city, than they perceived the importance of fuch a place, and prepared themfelves to render it a regular fortrefs. In about two months they completely furrounded it with earthen works and outworks, ditched and pallifadoed. Some of the neareft orchards were cut down to be ufed in thefe fortifications. The fruit trees ftill remain with their branches upwards from the ditch, and ferve inftead of *chevaux de frife*.

The village of Hockheim, which is alfo on this fide of the Rhine, is further to the left than Koftheim, and remains uninjured,

at

at the top of the round and easy hill, the vines of which are so much celebrated for their flavour, as to give a name to great quantities of wine, produced in other diſtricts. After the siege, the merchants of the neighbourhood enhanced the price of their stocks by reporting, that all the vineyards had been destroyed; but the truth is, that Hockheim was not much contended for, and that little damage was done even to the crops then in bloom. The village is advantageously situated about the confluence of the Rhine and the Maine, and, if it had been nearer the city, would probably have been so important, as to have been contested, till it was destroyed.

This is the home ground of the scene, which spreads before the traveller, who approaches Mentz from the eastern shore of the Rhine. Furthest to the left is Hockheim, then the devastated village of Koſtheim, then the fortifications of Caſſel, which,

which, with the river, are between him and the city. Beyond, the horizon is bounded on all sides by gradual hills, distant and apparently fruitful; but those to the north are pre-eminent, with gentle slopes at their feet, coloured sweetly by corn, dark wood and gleams of reddish earth.

The works of Caſſel render the approach to the city very tedious, for they have been so contrived as that the road nearly follows them, in all their angles, for the purpose of being commanded by many points at once. The village was now garrisoned by Pruſsians, of whom, some were lying under the sheds of their guard-house near the bridge, and others were riding over it, with just speed enough to give one an idea of military earnestness. Their horses shook the floor of the bridge of boats, which here crosses the Rhine, at its breadth of nearly eight hundred feet, and disturbed the promenade, for which it is usually frequented in an evening. We followed them, admiring the expanse, and rapidity of the river more than the appearance of the city, where gloominess is too much mingled with grandeur; till, at the end of the bridge, we were stopped at another guardhouse, to answer the usual enquiries. A soldier accompanied us thence to a large square filled with cannon and mortars, where the captain of the guard examined our passport. We were then very glad to pass the evening at an inn without further researches; but there were some symptoms of the late condition of the city to attract attention in the way.

The Elector's palace, which forms one side of this square, having been converted into an hospital by the French, is still used as such, or as a barrack, by the Prussians; and the windows were crowded with the figures of half-dressed soldiers. Many of the cannon in the square remained with

the

the fractures, made by the balls of the befiegers. This place communicates with a
broad street, in which were many buildings,
filled with foldiers, and an handfome houfe,
that, having belonged to one of the Club-
bifts, was deftroyed immediately after the
expulfion of the French. The walls ftill
remain bare and open. Some greater ruins,
occafioned by fire, during the fiege, were
vifible at a diftance; and, upon the whole,
we had intereft enough excited, as to the
immediate hiftory of the place, to take little
notice of the narrow and difficult paffages,
through which we wound for half an hour,
after leaving the principal ftreet.

The next morning, the friends, to whom
we had letters, began to conduct us through
the melancholy curiofities, left in the city
by the fiege. Thefe are chiefly in the
fouthern quarter, againft which the direct
attack of the allies was made, and their
approaches moft advanced. Some entire

streets

streets have been destroyed here, and were still in ruins. A magnificent church, attached to a convent of Franciscan monks, is among the most lamentable spectacles; what was the roof now lies in heaps over the pavement; not a vestige of furniture, or decoration, has escaped the flames, and there are chasms in the walls larger than the noble windows, that once illuminated them. This church and convent were set on fire by a bomb; and of the sick soldiers, who were lodged in the latter, it is feared that but few were removed before the destruction of the building. We next saw the remains of a palace, built by the present Provost of the Chapter of Nobles; an institution, which is so rich, that their Superior had a more elegant residence than the Elector. It was of stone, and the principal front was in the Corinthian order, six columns of which supported a spacious open gallery, ornamented with statues, for its whole

whole length. The wings formed two sides of a square, which separated the palace from the street. A profusion of the richest furniture and a valuable collection of paintings filled the interior. Of the whole edifice little now remains but the shattered walls of the centre, which have been so scorched as to lose all appearance of having belonged to a splendid structure. It was burnt the night before the fire of the Franciscan church, and two nights after the French had removed their head quarters and their municipality from it. On the day before the removal, a bomb had fallen upon the French General Blou, destroying him on the spot, and mortally wounding an officer, with whom he was conversing. The ruins are now so accumulated over the court-yard, that we could not discern it to have ever had that appendage of a distinguished residence.

But the church of Notre Dame was the

most

most conspicuous of many ruined objects. The steeple of this had been one of the grandest ornaments of the city; a shower of bombs set fire to it; and, while it was thus rendered an easy mark for the besiegers, their cannon played upon and beat a great part of it to the ground. By its fall the roof of the church was shattered, but the body did not otherwise suffer any material injury. Wooden galleries have been raised round the remainder of the steeple, not for the purpose of repairing, but for that of entirely removing it; and, to save the trouble of letting down the stones on the outside, a wooden pipe, or channel has been made, through which they are lowered into the church. The appearance of this steeple, which was once very large and lofty, is rendered striking by these preparations for its total destruction.

The whole church is built of a stone, dug from the neighbouring hills, the colour of which

which is so delicate a pink, that it might be supposed to be given by art. The Elector's palace and several other public buildings in the city are formed of this stone.

Passing through the gates on this side of Mentz, we came to a slope near the river, and beyond the glacis of the place, which was then partly covered with huge masses of stone scattered among the roots of broken trees and shrubs, that had begun again to shoot their verdure over the amputated trunks. This was the site of a palace of the Elector, called, both from the beauty of its situation, and the splendour of its structure, La Favorita. The apartments of the palace and the terraces of the garden commanded extensive views of the Rhine and the surrounding country ascending from its banks; and the gardens themselves were so beautifully disposed as to be thought worthy of the name of English. They were ornamented with pavilions, which had

Y   each

each its distinct prospect, and with one music room in the thickest part of the shrubbery. Of the building nothing is now visible but some disjointed stones; and of the garden, only the broken trunks of trees. The palace was burned and the gardens levelled by the French, that they might not afford shelter to the Prussians, during the siege.

From this spot we were shewn the positions of the allied forces, the course of their approaches and the chief outworks of the city. Höckheim, Kostheim and Cassel lay before us, on the other side of the river; a gentle rise on this side, at the distance of nearly a mile, was the first station of the allies, part of whose force was covered behind it; their last batteries were within two hundred and fifty paces of the city. The ground had been since levelled, and was now covered with standing corn, but the track of the trenches was, in some places, visible.

visible. On the other hand, the forts, in which the strength of the whole so much consists, were completely repaired, and had no appearance of having been so lately attacked. They are five in number, and, being raised at a considerable distance from the walls of the city, no near approaches can be made, till some of them are either taken, or destroyed; for they are said to be regular and strong fortifications, capable of containing numerous garrisons, and communicating with the city itself by passages, cut in the ground, through which they may be constantly reinforced.

Only one of these five forts, that nearest to the river, was destroyed in the late siege, which would have been much more tedious, but for the want of provisions and medicines, that began to be felt in the garrison. The walls of the city were almost uninjured, so that it has not been thought necessary to repair them in the few places, where balls may be perceived to have struck. The bombardment was the chief annoyance of the garrison, who were not sheltered in caserns, and whose magazines, both of ammunition and provision, were frequently destroyed by it. Their numbers were also greatly reduced by sallies and by engagements, on the other side of the Rhine, in defence of Cassel, or in attack of part of an island, called the Bleiau.

We walked round the city upon what is termed the *glacis*, that is upon the slope, which ascends from the plain towards the top of the ditch, and which is the furthest of the defensive works, being very gradually raised, that those, who are upon it, may be exposed, at every step, to the fire from the walls. The forts, which are formed of solid earthen works, covered with turf, would scarcely attract the notice of an unmilitary eye, if the channelled passages to them did not issue from this slope, and if the

the sentinels, stalking upon the parapets, did not seem of a gigantic size, by having their whole figures raised against the light.

Mentz was at this time the depôt of stores for the Prussian army on the Rhine, and there were persons employed upon the *glacis*, in counting heaps of cannon balls, which had been delivered from some neighbouring foundery. On the bank of the river, others were throwing waggon-loads of hay into large barges, on which it was piled to such an height, that small passages were cut through it for the rowers to work in. There were nine or ten barges so filled; and in these labours more activity was apparent than in any other transactions we saw at Mentz.

Having passed round the city, between the walls and the forts, which protect them, to the north, west and south, we came, at this latter side, to some other signals of a theatre of war. Here had been a noble

alley

alley of at least a mile and a half long, formed of poplars as large and high as elms, and furrounded, on each fide, by plantations, interfected by fmall and irregular walks. Being led along the banks of the Rhine, this alley, with its adjoining groves, afforded a moſt delightful promenade, and was claſſed amongſt the beſt ornaments, given to the river, in its whole courſe. This alſo was deſtroyed upon the approach of the beſiegers, that it might not afford them ſhelter. The trunks of the ſturdy trees, cut at the height of one or two feet from the ground, ſhew, by their ſolidity and the abundance of their vigorous ſhoots, how long they might have flouriſhed, but for this difaſter.

An Engliſhman, walking amidſt the enſigns of ſuch artificial and premature defolation, cannot help confidering the natural ſecurity of his country, and rejoicing, that, even if the ſtrong and plain policy of neglecting

glecting all foreign confequence, and avoiding all foreign interefts, except the commercial ones, which may be maintained by a navy, fhould for ever be rejected, ftill his home cannot be invaded; and, though the expence of wars fhould make poverty general, the immediate horrors of them cannot enter the cities, or the cottages of an ifland.

Great part of our time at Mentz was occupied by enquiries concerning the fiege, which was not fo much a topic as we had expected to find it. We probably heard, however, all that was to be told, and had a German pamphlet recommended, containing the hiftory of the place from the firft invafion of the French to their departure. The authenticity of this was affured to us; and it is partly from it, partly from the accounts given by our friends, that the following fhort narrative has been extracted.

GERMANY.

OF MENTZ IN 1792 AND 1793.

THE entrance of a French army into Worms, in the beginning of October 1792, had excited a confiderable alarm in Mentz, before the inhabitants of the latter city received the accounts, which were not long wanting, of exprefs and avowed preparations for a march towards them. Great numbers of French emigrants had been drawn to the city by the meeting of the Emperor and the King of Pruffia there, a few months before; many had arrived fince the diffolution of their army in Champagne; and, during the approach of the Republican troops to Spires and Worms, families were continually paffing through the city, joining thofe, who began to take their flight from it. The narrow ftreets were filled with carriages, and the diftrefsful hafte of the travellers ferved to deprefs the

the spirits of the inhabitants, who saw how little their city was thought capable of defence. On the 15th of October, Baron d'Albini, a counsellor of the Court, called the Burgesses together, and admonished them to make preparations for their security; he also enquired, whether they thought it prudent, that the Elector should remain in the city with them? and, it being readily answered, that they did not, the Elector set out for Wurtzburg, a town about 100 miles distant, and was followed by the members of the government. At the same time, a considerable emigration of the other inhabitants took place.

The approach of the French had been so little foreseen, till within the few last weeks, that the garrison did not amount to a tenth part of the war complement. The inhabitants, however, having happily had little experience of sieges, did not know what this complement should be, and, after the first alarm,

alarm, began to think the deficiency might be eafily remedied. The Electoral troops, having fent fome ufelefs detachments to Spires, amounted to only 968 men, to whom an hundred were added, obtained from Naffau, Oranien, Weilburg, Bieberich and Fuld by the Elector's demands of affiftance from his neighbours. Two hundred and feven Auftrian huffars of Efterhazy had alfo arrived, on the 13th, and all the inhabitants of the Rheingau, a populous diftrict, bordering upon the Rhine, were fummoned to the affiftance of the capital. The antient fociety of Archers of the city laid down their bows for mufquets; the Academicians formed themfelves into a corps, and were placed, together with the Archers, at feveral outpofts. The traders, though exempt from perfonal fervice, and unwilling to furrender that privilege, refolved to pay double watch-money for fubftitutes. It began to be thought, that the threatened progrefs progress of the French had been untruly reported; that the siege could not be commenced at that late season of the year; and lastly, that some promised reinforcements of Austrian troops could not be far off.

But, on the 19th of October, the French, in four columns, began to surround the place. They wore, at first, white cockades, expecting to be mistaken for the army of M. de Condé; they were, however, known, and fired upon. Though some days had been passed in preparation, it was now found, that there was little readiness for defence. The best artillerymen had been lost at Spires; there were, at first, no horses to draw the cannon, so that oxen were used for that purpose; the nearest balls to the batteries of twenty-four pound cannon were cast for twelve-pounders; and many of the musquet cartridges could not be fired. In a few hours, however, several of the artisans applied themselves to the making of cartridges;

cartridges; horses were supplied by the servants of the Court and the Nobility, and all hands were, in some way or other, employed. It was then reported, that a corps of Austrian troops was in the neighbourhood, and, on the 19th, 1800 men entered the city. These were recruits without ammunition, and, for the most part, without arms, being on their march to join the army of the Emperor. They were then under the command of two or three subalterns; but some other Imperial officers came in from the neighbourhood, and arms were obtained from the Elector's arsenal. After this reinforcement there were probably about four thousand men in arms in the city.

With this force, it is allowed, that a much longer defence than was made might have been expected; and, unless there was some failure of the commander's attention, the treachery of an engineer, to whom the surrender

surrender is imputed, could certainly not have been so effectual. EIKENMAYER, this engineer, had, it seems, made known to the French the commander's preparations for defence; intelligence, which, if the preparations had been greater, could have been but little serviceable to the assailants. His chief assistance was afforded to them by much more conspicuous means; for, as the inhabitants went frequently to a building called St. Stephen's Tower, to observe the progress of the besiegers, he assured them, that the army, which really amounted only to eleven thousand men, consisted of forty thousand; that they had with them two-and-twenty waggons, laden with scaling ladders, and that the city would presently be taken by storm. The same representations of the besiegers' force were also made by him to the Council of War; and these, it is said, determined them to the surrender,

before

before the French had raised a battery against the works.

Many of the citizens, however, were surprised and enraged at this resolution; and the captain of the Austrian reinforcements expressed his displeasure, at the Council House, where he declared, that he would continue to defend the place, even without permission. In the mean time, the capitulation was signed, and he was induced to submit to it by the solicitations even of the citizens, by whom it was blamed, and by their representations, that, in the present agitated temper of the inhabitants, all attempts at defence must be useless.

Baron d'ALBINI carried news of the surrender to the Elector, at Wurtzburg, and, about five o'clock, on the 21st of October, two French officers came to the Council House, followed by two companies of grenadiers. On the 22d, eight thousand French
entered

entered the city, the other three thouſand having marched, the preceding day, to Franckfort; the inhabitants, aſtoniſhed to find themſelves taken by ſo ſmall a force, now ſaw, to their ſtill greater ſurpriſe, that their conquerors had ſcarcely any heavy cannon. This day was paſſed in aſſigning quarters to the troops, and, on the next, Cuſtine, the commander of the French, called the members of the City Council together, to whom, in a ſhort ſpeech, he promiſed the protection of perſons and properties, inviting them, at the ſame time, to promote the fraternization of the inhabitants with the French nation. Profeſſor BOHMER, who had accepted the office of his Secretary, tranſlated this addreſs into German, and it was circulated through the city.

It is remarkable, that the French had no ſooner taken poſſeſſion of this ſudden prize, than they began to foreſee the probability
of

of being reduced to defensive measures, and to prepare for them. They immediately collected contributions of forage and corn from the neighbouring villages; the streets were rendered almost impassable by the loads brought in; and, as the magazines were soon filled, great quantities were wasted by being exposed to the rain in gardens, and trodden under the feet of horses in the streets. The garrison was soon increased to 20,000 men, of whom sometimes three hundred sometimes five hundred were lodged in each convent. The French soldiery having committed some excesses, Custine reproved their licentiousness, and began to habituate them to discipline by ordering a retirement to their quarters, at certain hours, by beat of drum.

The inhabitants soon began to suspect the contrivance and the persons, that had produced the surrender; for Eikenmayer lived in intimacy with Custine; Professor for Metternich, of the Academy of Mentz, mounted the French cockade; and the Elector's phyſician, having left the city, upon a promiſe of aſſiſting ſome peaſants, whom he aſſerted to be ſeized with an infectious fever, had carried on a correſpondence with the French, as had PATOKI, a merchant, born at Colmar, who had lately received the right of citizenſhip.

The palaces of the Elector and the Provoſt were now ranſacked; and, though it had been publiſhed as a rule, that the property of private individuals ſhould not be touched, the houſes of the nobility were treated, as if they had belonged to the Prince. The profligacy and pride of Cuſtine became every day more conſpicuous, and were oppreſſive upon the garriſon, as well as the inhabitants, though in a leſs degree. Johanneſberg, a village upon the Rhine, at the diſtance of a few miles, is celebrated for its wines, which fell for

three

three times the price of those of Hockheim. Custine sent a part of the garrison solely to bring him the wines from the cellars of the Prince of Fuld, who has a palace there; but, a compromise being proposed, the negotiation was protracted so long, that a Prussian corps, for which the Prince had sent, carried Johannesberg, before the terms were concluded. The Prince saved his money, and lost only eighteen barrels of wine, of which part was sent to Paris, and the rest supplied the entertainments given by Custine.

Those of the Germans, who attached themselves to Custine, supplied him with information of the state of the whole country. His Secretary, Professor Bohmer, had begun the institution of a Club so early as the 22d of October; but this society is thought to have become inconvenient, and they soon after began to prepare for a National Convention in Mentz.

In

In the mean time, Caffel was furveyed, and the fortifications, for which Eikenmayer is faid to have furnifhed the defign, were commenced. The neighbouring peafants were fummoned to work at thefe, at the price of fifteen French fous, or about feven pence halfpenny a day; and intrenchments were thrown round Koftheim.

On the 17th of December, Cuftine publifhed a proclamation, in which he ftated, that, whereas fome perfons had fuppofed the King of Pruffia to have fo little refpect for his character as to have invited him to a furrender, none fhould prefume, on pain of death, to fpeak of fuch a meafure, in future. This proclamation gave the inhabitants of Mentz information, that the Pruffians were approaching. Some German troops had, indeed, begun by degrees to occupy the ground about Coblentz, but in a condition, which did not promife active meafures, being weakened by a long march and by sickness; the Hessians posted themselves between Hanau and Franckfort; and the Prussians advanced so near to the latter city, that the scattered parties of the French retired to, and at length lost it.

About this time, an Electoral Professor of Philosophy and a Canon of Mentz, named Dorsel, who had left his posts, in the preceding year, to be naturalized, at Strasbourg, returned with a design for an union of Spires, Worms and Mentz into one territory, under the protection of the French. He procured the substitution of a Municipality for the City Council. He obtained considerable influence in the city; and, on the 1st of January 1793, when the three Commissioners of the Convention, Reubell, Merlin and Haussman, entered Mentz, and were received by Custine with military honours, they shewed more attention to the Professor than to the General.

The Prussian head quarters had been
eftablished

established within a short distance of Mentz; but, during all December, there had been only affairs of advanced posts, so that some tranquillity prevailed in the city. On the 6th of January, Hockheim was assailed by six thousand Prussians; the French, however, had been informed of the preparations for attack, and had time to retire to Kostheim and Cassel, leaving 112 prisoners and twelve pieces of cannon. Some French, who had concealed themselves in the church tower, were thrown headlong from it, for having shouted, or thrown stones, at the King of Prussia, as he passed.

After this, another month passed, without hostile attempts on either side. The Prussian troops were refreshed by rest; the French passed the same time, partly in balls, to which all the ladies of Mentz were invited, and partly in preparations for defence. On the 17th of January, a small tree of liberty, which had been planted in

November, was removed, and a fir, seventy feet high, placed in its stead, with much ceremony. All the inhabitants were pressingly invited, upon this occasion; Messrs. Reubell, Merlin, Haussman and Custine attended; the Mayor, Municipality, and the Members of the Clubs followed; the ensigns of the former government were burned; Custine called upon the music of the garrison for French airs, which occupied the rest of the day; and the evening concluded with entertainments and dancing. Soon after, the Commissioners left the city, and proceeded on a journey to the Moselle.

On the 16th of February, Custine published a proclamation, and two new Commissioners, who had just arrived, issued another, founded upon a decree of the French Convention, relative to the union of other countries with France. The Council House was full from morning till night; the assembled traders declared their adherence

herence to the Germanic fyftem; and the new Commiffioners feemed inclined to liften to their remonftrances. But, when the three former Commiffioners returned, they treated the Deputies of the trades with great haughtinefs, and refufed them permiffion to fend agents to Paris. A fecond deputation, on the 22d of February, was no better received, and they were informed, that the 24th was the day for the commencement of the new form. The traders are defcribed to have been much affected, at the return of their Deputies. On the 23d of February, early in the morning, the author of a remonftrance, which had been prefented, was arrefted and carried into banifhment, being accompanied by guards to the advanced pofts of the Pruffians, at Hockheim.

The inhabitants now began to leave the city by paffports, which were, however, not

eafily

GERMANY.

easily procured, or used. A proclamation by the Municipality divided Mentz into sections, and directed the manner, in which each section should elect a representative, on the 24th. On that day, the streets were unusually silent, all the former burgesses having resolved to remain in their houses, except one, and only 266 persons met to take the new oath; and to make the new elections. On the 25th, another proclamation came out, and several banishments succeeded; but the burgesses still adhered to their resolution. The Municipality, on the 1st of March, again invited them to take the new oaths, and gave notice of an order of the Commissioners to the Mayor, to publish a list of the sworn and unsworn, on the Monday or Tuesday following. Notwithstanding this, the number of sworn did not equal 350.

Some of the neighbouring villages, which were

were visited by the French Commissioners, accepted their terms; the greater part refused them.

At Worms, where clubs, similar to those at Mentz, had been formed, 1051 persons took the oaths. The inhabitants of Bingen refused them.

In the mean time, some expeditions were made into the Palatinate, and corn, to the amount of sixty thousand florins, was taken away, before the reiterated remonstrances of the Palatine Resident at Mentz, upon the subject of his master's neutrality, could restrain them. In the first days of February, the French had also entered Deux Ponts, where the Duke relied so much upon his having supplied only his contingent to the treasure of the Empire, that he had not left his palace, though he knew of their approaches to his country. On the 9th, at eleven at night, the Duke and Duchess fled, with the utmost precipitation, to Manheim,

having

having left the palace only one hour before the French entered it. Great quantities of forage were swept away from this country, and brought to Mentz, which the allies now approached so nearly, that the garrison hastily completed the fortifications of Cassel, and filled the magazines with stores, lest the communication should be cut off by the destruction of the bridge.

On the 15th of February, they had begun to destroy the palace of *La Favorita*, and to erect a battery upon its ruins. Though the carriage of provisions now occupied so much of their attention, a great number of large and small cannon were brought from Landau; fresh troops arrived, and General Wimpfen, who had defended Thionville against the King of Prussia, was declared the first in command. By banishments and emigration, the number of persons in the city was reduced fifteen thousand.

GERMANY.

The new National Assembly met in Mentz, on the 10th of March, that city having chosen six deputies, Spires two, Worms two, and some other places one each. On the 17th, they had their first sitting, and, on the 18th, declared all the country between Landau and Bingen, which places were then the limits of the French posts near the Rhine, united in one independent state. On the 19th, was agitated the great question relative to the connections of this state, and it was not till the 21st, that they declared their incorporation with the French. Three deputies, FORSTER, PATOKI and LUCKS were appointed, the next day, to carry this resolution to Paris; and several decrees, relative to the interior administration of this state, were passed, in consequence of which many persons were conducted over the bridge into banishment, on the 30th.

Accounts now arrived, that the siege would

would shortly commence, and orders were issued, relative to the prevention of fires, to the collection of stores, of provisions by each family, and, to several other domestic particulars. All the inhabitants, those especially in the neighbourhood of the granaries, were directed to preserve large quantities of water; and the proprietors of gardens within the city were ordered to plant them with herbs. Officers were sent round to examine these gardens. Already each family had been admonished to provide subsistence for seven months; and the richer class were now directed to furnish a loan to the burgesses, that the latter might be enabled to provide for the poor. In consequence of this order, 38,646 florins 10 creitzers, or about 3200 l., were collected and expended for provisions. The gardens and walks round the city were now dismantled of their trees, of which those in the *Rheinallee*, before mentioned, were an

hundred

hundred years old. All the summer-houses and villas, within cannon shot of the city, were destroyed.

On the 8th of March, the French garrison in the fortress of Konigstein, which the Prussians had blockaded for some months, surrendered. In this month also other advances were made towards Mentz. The Prussian General Schonfield brought 12,000 men into the neighbourhood of Hockheim, near which the Saxons were posted; the King of Prussia, his son and the Duke of Brunswick, who had passed part of the winter at Franckfort, left it, on the 23d of March; a bridge was laid, at St. Goar, over which numerous bodies of Prussian troops passed the Rhine; the French fell back towards Bingen, and the Prussians occupied a hill, not far from it. On the 28th, they were closer pressed, and left all the villages in the neighbourhood of Bingen,

from

from which place they were driven, the next day, by a bombardment.

At the same time, a similar retreat towards Mentz also took place from the southward. At Worms, during the abandonment, great quantities of hay and straw were burned, and the burgesses kept watch, all night, dreading the conflagration of the whole city by the flames, rising from the magazines. Immense masses of hay and straw were also burned at Frankenthal, where there had been a garrison, during the whole winter; but the corn was carried away. At Spires, early on the 31st of March, the burgesses and troops were employed in throwing the hay and straw from the magazines into the ditch; but it appeared that even this mode would not be expeditious enough, and fire was at length set to the whole store at once.

In the retreat from Oppenheim, though the

the French were under confiderable difficulties, they were upon the point of obtaining what they would have thought an abundant reward for them. It was on the 30th of March, that their cavalry and flying artillery took the road by Alfheim. As this was a place capable of making fome defence, and there were Pruffian troops vifible at the gates, they began the attack by planting cannon, and directing a vigorous fire upon it. The King of Pruffia, who was at dinner in the town, and had not an hundred men with him, received his firft intelligence of their approach from this fire. He immediately rode out, on the oppofite fide, and, fending fome huffars to the fpot, the French did not continue the conteft, but made their retreat by another road. If they had known how few troops were in the town, they would, of courfe, have entered it without commencing this fire; and the Pruffian officers agree, that, if they

had

had done so, there would have been little chance of saving their monarch. Had they been aware also, that his Prussian Majesty was there, they might have reduced this slight chance to an impossibility; for they were sufficiently numerous to have surrounded the town, and had approached so quietly, that they were not known to be near it. The Prussians had no cannon, and the French were otherwise greatly superior; though, having no other purpose for entering the town, than to continue their retreat, they did not wait to contest it, but retired by another road. That a circumstance, which would have had such an effect upon the affairs of Europe, should have depended upon so slight a chance as this, we could not have believed, if the story had not been confirmed to us by ample authority.

The garrison of Mentz was increased by these retreats to 23,000 men; General Kalkreuth,

kreuth, who commanded the blockade from Laubenheim to Budenheim, a distance of twelve miles, had only 16,000 men. General Schonfield, with his corps of obfervation, was at Hockheim. The besiegers, however, prefently amounted to 30,000 men. It is remarkable, that, though the French retreated from several quarters, at once, and in many small columns, not one of these was effectually interrupted by the Pruffian commander.

Upon intelligence of these advances, the Elector of Mentz paid a vifit to the King of Pruffia, at his head quarters, and left his minifter, the Baron d'ALBINI, to attend to the affairs of the recovered places.

In the beginning of April, the blockade was more clofely preffed, and the preparations for the fiege ferioufly commenced. General d'OYRE was made commander in the city, with a Council of fixteen perfons,

A a to

to assist him in restoring the means of its defence. A person was placed at the top of an high building, called Stephen's Tower, with glasses, which enabled him to overlook the country for nine miles round. He had a secretary with him, that his view might never be unnecessarily diverted, and was obliged to make a daily report of his observations. The beating of drums and ringing of bells were forbidden throughout the whole city, that the besiegers might not know in what quarters the corps de garde were placed, or what churches were left without the military. All prospect houses and trees within the walls, which could serve as marks to the fire without, were ordered to be demolished. Many days were passed in bringing further stores of provisions into the city; after which an account of the stock was taken, and there were found to be

24,090

GERMANY.

  24,090 facks of wheat.
   1,465   of other corn.
   996   of mixed grain.

Of which 26,551 facks, it was ftated, that 23,070 facks of meal could be made. To this was to be added in fifted meal of wheat 109 facks, of other corn 45 facks, of mixed grain 10,076 facks; making in all 33,300 facks of meal. There were befides

  43,960 rations of bifcuit.
   7,275 pounds of rice.
  13,045   of dried herbs.

Of forage, 10,820 quintals of hay.

  54,270   of ftraw.
   1,518 facks of oats.
   2,503   of barley.

The Council eftimated, that the garrifon had corn enough for nine months, rice for feven, and herbs for fix. There were fifteen hundred horfes, and it was reckoned, that the straw was enough for ten months, the oats for four-and-twenty days, and the barley for eighty days. The garrison was numbered, and found to consist of 22,653 persons; of whom to each soldier was allotted, for the future, 24 ounces of bread, per day, in lieu of 28, and 4 ounces of fresh meat, or 3 ounces of salt, in lieu of 8 ounces of fresh. The allowance of the sick in the hospitals was changed from twelve to eight ounces.

During these preparations for a long siege, the diminution of the number of inhabitants, by means of the clubs, was pursued. On the 8th of April, all persons, not useful to the army, were ordered to leave the city, unless they would take the new oath; at the same time, it was said, that on account of the foreseen want of money, the soldiers, employed on the works, would be no longer paid, but the other workmen would continue to receive their salaries.

The

GERMANY.

The garrison made their first sortie, on the night of the 10th and 11th, proceeding towards the Rhine. Kostheim was immediately taken, and the attack upon the Hessians succeeded, at first, but a reinforcement compelled the French to retire. About this time, the Commissioner Reubell went to Oppenheim, where he delivered a proposal for peace to the King of Prussia.

The village of Weissenau was contended for, on the 15th, 16th and 17th, and finally destroyed, the French soldiers, who remained upon the spot, subscribing 460 livres for the inhabitants.

On the 18th, nearly the whole of a French convoy of 90 waggons was taken by the Prussians. On the 20th the Imperialists erected a small fort on a point of land, near the Main, and the French, on the other hand, perfected a battery, at Kostheim, with which they set on fire some stables.

The price of provisions was already so much increased in the city, that salt butter cost 48 creitzers, or 16d. pence per pound.

In the night of the 28th and 29th, the French landed in three vessels, and destroyed a battery, erected near the Main. On the 1st of May, at one in the morning, they attacked the Prussians, at Hockheim, and set the village of Kostheim on fire. The Prussians repulsed them with loss, but they remained in Kostheim, notwithstanding the fire, which continued for three days ; they were then expelled by the Prussians, but soon returned with reinforcements, and a sanguinary contest commenced, at the end of which they continued to be masters of the village. A numerous garrison was placed in it, which, on the 8th, was again attacked by the Prussians, but without effect. Thus the greatest part of May was spent in contests for villages and posts, in which the French were generally

nerally the affailants. In the night of the 30th, they beat up, in three columns, the Pruffian head quarters, at Marienborn. Having marched barefooted and with such exact information, that they paffed all the batteries unperceived, they entered the village itfelf, without refiftance, and, it is fuppofed, would have furprifed the commander, if they had not fired at his windows, beat their drums, and begun to fhout *Vive la Nation!* Three balls, which entered the apartment of General KALKREUTH, admonifhed him to quit it, and a fentinel ftepped up juft in time to fhoot a French foldier, who had feized him. Prince Louis Ferdinand of Pruffia immediately arrived with fome troops, and the French began to retire, leaving thirty prifoners and twenty killed of 6000, engaged in the enterprife. The lofs of the Pruffians was confiderable; amongft the reft Captain Vofs, a relative of Mademoiselle Voſs, well known in the Court of Pruſſia.

On the 4th of June, the allowance to the garriſon was ordered to be two pounds of bread and one bottle of wine for each ſoldier, per day.

In the night of the 6th and 7th, the cannonade was very fierce, on both ſides; in Mentz a powder magazine was fired by a bomb, and blew up with a dreadful exploſion.

The ſcarceneſs of proviſions increaſed, ſo that a pound of freſh butter coſt ſix ſhillings. Horſefleſh began to be conſumed in many families.

On the night of the 9th and 10th of June, the garriſon made four ſorties, which ended in conſiderable loſs, on both ſides, and in the retirement of the French into the city. On the 10th, they attacked, at eight in the morning, a poſt near Gonſenheim, retreating without loſs, after killing an an officer and several men. This was their first sally in open day-light.

General Meusnier, who had been wounded near Caffel, on the 7th, died on the 13th, and was buried the next day, within the new fortifications, all the officers of the garrison, with the members of the convention and clubs, attending.

Some fire ships were now completed, which a Dutch engineer had conducted from Holland, to be employed by the besiegers in burning the bridge of boats over the Rhine. It was thought, however, that their explosion would damage the city unnecessarily, and they were rejected. In the night of the 15th, one of these floated down the river, whether by accident, or by the connivance of the inventor, is not known; the inhabitants were in the utmost terror, but it struck against the quay, and, being immediately boarded, did no damage.

The trenches were opened, in the night of

of the 16th and 17th, but, the workmen having been ill conducted, were not covered in, at day-light, and were compelled to retire, leaving their implements behind them. Two nights afterwards, the work was renewed in good order and without lofs, the King of Pruffia, his fons and the Duke of Brunfwick furveying them from a neighbouring height. The firft balls fell in a ftreet near one of the gates, and all that part of the town was prefently deferted.

The 24th was a diftrefsful day for the inhabitants. Four days before, the King of Pruffia had fent a general paffport for fuch as chofe to come out, and 1500 perfons, chiefly women and children, had accepted his offer. A fhort time after the gate had been opened, difmay was fpread through the whole city by an account, that the Pruffians would fuffer no more to pafs and the French none to return. The bridge was covered with thefe unhappy fugitives, who had

had no food, or shelter, and who thought themselves within reach of the Hockheim batteries, that played furiously upon the city. Two children lost their senses through fright. At length, the French soldiers took compassion upon them; they carried several persons into the city under their cloaks, and, the next day, their remonstrances against the inhumanity of the German clubbists, who had shut the gates against this defenceless crowd, obliged them to permit the return of the whole number.

For several succeeding nights, the garrison made sorties, with various effect, interrupting, but not preventing the completion of the parallel.

At sunset, on the 27th, the besiegers began a dreadful cannonade and bombardment. On this night, the steeple of the church of Notre Dame caught fire; and during the alarm, excited by an immense volume of flame, arising in the midst of the

the city, the Austrians completely carried the French posts, near Weissenau. The next night was equally terrible to the inhabitants; the flames caught several parts of the city, amongst others the cathedral; some of the magazines took fire, and eleven hundred sacks of corn were burned. The church, formerly belonging to the Jesuits, was much injured. The French, intending to retaliate their last surprise upon the Austrians, made a fruitless attack upon the Weissenau redoubt.

On the 29th of June, at mid-day, the French were driven from a point of land, near the Main, called the Bleiau. In this affair, a vessel, with 78 Prussians on board, drove from her anchor, owing to the unskilfulness of the crew, and, during a fire, by which eight men were killed, made towards the city. The Prussians were taken prisoners, and exchanged the next day. At night, the bombardment was renewed; the

Domprobstei,

Domprobſtei, or palace of the Provoſt, was burned and ſeveral of the neighbouring reſidences; in other parts of the city, ſome houſes were reduced to aſhes.

The next night, the church of the Franciſcans and ſeveral other public buildings were deſtroyed. A dreadful fire, on the night of the 2d and 4th of June, conſumed the chapel of St. Alban. Families in the ſouthern part of the city now conſtantly paſſed the night in their cellars; in the day-time, they ventured into their uſual apartments; for the batteries of the beſiegers were by far the moſt terrible, at night, when the whole city was a ſufficient mark for them, though their works could ſcarcely be diſcerned by the garriſon. In the day-time, the exactneſs of the French gunners frequently did great injury to the batteries, which, at night, were repaired and uſed with equal effect againſt the city.

St. Alban's fort was now demoliſhed, ſo that

that the befieged withdrew their cannon from it. Elizabeth fort was alfo much damaged. A ftrong work, which the French had raifed, in prolongation of the *glacis*, divided the opinions of the Pruffian engineers. Some thought it fhould be preferved, when taken, becaufe it would command part of the town; others, that it fhould be demolifhed. The latter opinion prevailed, and, in the night of the 5th and 6th, General MANSTEIN was ordered to make the attack with three battalions. He perfectly fucceeded, as to the neareft part of the work; but the other, on account of its folid foundation, could not be entirely deftroyed. In the mean time, two battalions were fent, under cover of the darknefs, to attack the Zahlbach fort, a part of which they carried by ftorm; but the reinforcements, immediately fupplied by the garrifon, obliged them to retire. Two Pruffian officers were killed; one wounded, and another

another, with one-and-thirty men, taken. The Pruſſians loſt in all 183 men; the French had twelve killed and forty-ſeven wounded.

On the 6th of July, the French repaired the damaged fort, the diſtance of it from the Pruſſians preventing the latter from hindering them.

At night, General Kleiſt carried the fort, at Zahlbach, by a ſecond attack, and demoliſhed it; at the ſame time, ſome batteries of the ſecond parallel were perfected. The French could not ſupport the loſs of this fort; on the 7th, they attacked the ſcite; carried it, after a ſevere conteſt; and rebuilt it. At night, they were driven back again and the fort entirely deſtroyed. In the ſame night they were driven from Koſtheim, after a furious battle, by the Pruſſian General Schonfield. During this engagement, the rapid ſucceſſion of flaſhes and exploſion of bombs ſeemed to fill the

air

air with flame. A Prussian detachment having been posted on the road to Cassel, in order to prevent the garrison of that place from sending succour to Kostheim, this road was so strongly bombarded by the French, that seven bombs were frequently seen in the air at once. The loss was great, on both sides, in this engagement, after which the Council in the city resolved, to make no more attempts upon Kostheim, on account of the distance.

The following night, the fire was less than usual, but a few bombs and grenades fell in the city, where the inhabitants had now learned to extinguish such as grounded, before their *fusees* were consumed. They also formed themselves into parties for the ready suppression of fires. The next morning, the garrison saw the works of the besiegers brought to within two hundred and fifty paces of the walls.

About this time, the sickliness of the garrison

rifon became apparent, and General d'Oyré informed the Council, that, on account of this and of the fatiguing fervice of the works, he feared the defence could not be much longer continued. He lamented, that the troops of the line were fo few, and the others fo inexperienced.

For feveral nights, the works of the befiegers were eagerly pufhed, but ftill they were not fo forward, as had been expected. Some of the befieging corps began to be fickly; the King of Pruffia having refolved to employ no more labourers, it was reckoned, that the foldiers, for eight-and-forty hours of work, had only eighteen of reft. On the other hand, they were affured, that the garrifon muft be equally fatigued, fince, in fuch an extenfive fortification, none could be left long unemployed.

The French had been, for fome time, bufied in forming what is called a Fleche at the head of one of their forts, and this was

B b   thought

thought necessary to be destroyed. It was attacked in the night of the 12th and 13th by the Austrians; but so much time was passed in their operations, that the French fell upon them, in great force, about two in the morning, and beat them away, with loss. The Austrians were as little employed as possible in services of this sort.

On the 13th of July, another battery was stormed by the Prussians; but, as the officer, unlike the Austrians, advanced with too little caution, his party was much hurt by some pieces of concealed cannon, and the enterprise failed.

The night of the 13th and 14th was passed in much agitation by the garrison and inhabitants. Several of the public buildings were set fire to and burned by grenades. The works of the besiegers were now greatly advanced. The garrison made five sorties in this night, and were repulsed in all, losing an hundred men, while the besiegers

besiegers lost eight killed and one-and-thirty wounded.

On the 14th of July, a cessation of arms took place from seven o'clock in the morning till one. In the city, the French celebrated their annual fête; General d'OYRE and the troops took the oath, and MERLIN delivered an address to them. In the Austrian camp, the Prince de CONDE was received with a *feu de joye*. During this cessation, the soldiers upon the different outposts entered into conversation with each other, and the French boasted of the difficulties they laboured under from the length of the siege.

At night, an affair at the Fleche cost the allies, who succeeded in part, ninety men; the French confessed, that this work cost them in all three hundred. The inhabitants of the city were again greatly alarmed, their streets being covered with a shower of grenades. The laboratory and a part of the Benedictine abbey were burned, and two explosions took place at the former. The whole city shook with each report, and, in the nearer parts, all the windows were broken and the doors burst open. The remainder of the hay and straw was consumed in this fire; the whole stock of other forage was reduced to a sufficiency for four days; and the surgeon's stores were much damaged.

Still the Fleche prevented the besiegers from completing their second parallel. It was, therefore, again attacked, on the night of the 16th and 17th, Prince Louis Ferdinand of Prussia commanding at the assault, in which he was one of twelve officers wounded. The Fleche was then completely carried.

The next night was very industriously spent by the besiegers in forming new batteries, and those of the second parallel were raised, before there were cannon enough at hand

GERMANY.

hand to place upon them. The French took advantage of this, and brought a part of theirs to bear, so as to enfilade the parallel, with great effect; the Prussians almost immediately losing an officer and forty men.

In the city, the sick had now increased so much, that six hundred men were brought from Cassel, on the 17th, to reinforce the garrison. On the 18th, the commandant informed the Council, that there was a want of fodder and such a loss of horses, by desertion, that there were not cavalry enough left for service. The soldiers, who knew the deficiency of medicines and other means of relief for the wounded, were unwilling to be led to sorties. Though corn had not failed, flour, it appeared, soon would, for some of the mills had been rendered unserviceable, for the present, by shot, and others were deserted by the millers.

At night, after an unsuccessful attempt upon the Fleche, it was resolved, that the garrison,

garrison, which had hitherto scarcely suffered a night to pass, without making some sorties, should, for the future, adhere solely to defensive measures. Some engineers proposed to abandon the whole line of forts, and others, that two of the largest should be blown up. The General and Council, at length, confessed, that they could not continue the defence, and assured the inhabitants, who had declared themselves in their favour, that a longer delay of the surrender would produce a more severe disposition of the besiegers towards them, without increasing the chance of escaping it.

A negotiation, relative to the surrender, was now begun by D'OYRE, in a letter, which partly replied to one from the Prussian commander KALKREUTH, upon the subject of the departure of aged persons and children from the city. Their correspondence continued till the 20th, and several letters were exchanged, chiefly upon the question

question of the removal, or detention of the inhabitants, who had attached themselves to the French; it was then broken off, upon a disagreement, as to this and some other points. The firing, on both sides, had in the mean time continued, and the besiegers carried on the trenches, though these were now such an easy mark for the garrison, that they lost an officer and five-and-twenty men, in the night of the 19th and 20th. The next night, the Dominicans' church in the city took fire, and six French soldiers were buried under its ruins.

Upon a renewal of the intercourse, the fire slackened, on the 21st; but, on some delays in the negotiation, was threatened to be recommenced. At length, the conditions of the surrender were settled, and the negotiation signed, on the 22d of July, by the two Generals Kalkreuth and D'Oyré; the former having rendered the capitulation somewhat easier than was expected for the garrison, garrifon, becaufe the Duke of Brunfwick had only nineteen thoufand men to cover the fiege, and Cuftine had forty thoufand, which were near enough to attack him. General KALKREUTH's orders are fuppofed to have been to obtain poffeffion of the place, upon any terms, that would give it him quickly.

At this time, the garrifon, which, at the commencement of the fiege, had confifted of 22,653 men, was reduced to 17,038, having had 1959 killed, 3334 wounded, or rendered unferviceable by ficknefs, and having loft 322 by defertion.

The lofs of the befiegers is ftated at about 3000 men.

The confumption of ammunition, on the part of the French, was found to have been

681,850 pounds of powder,
106,152 cannon balls,
10,278 bombs,
6592 grenades,

44,400

44,500 pounds of iron,

300,340 mufquet cartridges;

and, during the fiege, 107 cannon either burft, or were rendered unferviceable by the befiegers' fhot. Towards the conclufion, fixty cannon alfo became ufelefs by the failure of balls of the proper calibre.

On the 24th and 25th, the garrifon marched out, MERLIN leading the firft column of 7500 men. The members of the Clubs, who would have gone out with the troops, were pointed out by the other inhabitants and detained; but the Elector had the magnanimity to think of no other retaliation, than their imprifonment in a tower, near the Rhine, where they have fince remained.

There was now leifure to examine the city, and it was found, that fix churches were in ruins; that feven manfions of the nobility had been burned, and that very few houfes had efcaped, without fome damage.

The

The surrounding grounds were torn up by balls and batteries. The works of Caffel were surrendered entire to the conquerors, and are an important addition to the strength of Mentz, already reckoned one of the strongest and largest fortifications in Europe. Between Caffel and the ruins of Koftheim not a tree was to be seen. All the neighbouring villages were more, or less, injured, being contended for, as posts, at the commencement of the siege; and the country was so much disfigured, that the proprietors of lands had some difficulty to ascertain their boundaries.

MENTZ.

SOMETHING has been already said of the present condition of this city: upon a review it appears, that from the mention of churches, palaces, burgesses, quays and streets,

streets, we might be supposed to represent it as a considerable place, either for splendour, or commerce, or for having its middle classes numerously filled. Any such opinion of Mentz will be very incorrect. After two broad and somewhat handsome streets, all the other passages in the city are narrow lanes, and into these many of the best houses open, having, for the most part, their lower windows barricadoed, like those of Cologne. The disadvantage, with which any buildings must appear in such situations, is increased by the neglected condition of these; for a German has no notion, that the outside of his house should be clean, even if the inside is so. An Englishman, who spends a few hundred pounds in a year, has his house in better condition, as to neatness, than any German nobleman's we saw; a Dutchman, with fifty pounds a year, exceeds both.

The Elector's palace is a large turreted building of reddish stone, with one front
towards

towards the Rhine, which it commands in a delightful point of view; but we did not hear, that it was so much altered, by being now used as a barrack, as that its appearance can formerly have been much less suitable than at present to such a purpose.

On the quay there is some appearance of traffic, but not much in the city; so that the transfer of commodities from vessels of other districts to those of the Electorate may be supposed to contribute great part of the show near the river. The commerce is not sufficient to encourage the building of warehouses over the quay. The vessels are ill rigged, and the hulls are entirely covered with pitch, without paint. About thirty of these, apparently from forty to seventy tons burthen, were lying near the quay; and the war could scarcely have diminished their usual number, so many being employed in carrying stores for the armies.

The burgesses are numerous, and have some

GERMANY.

some privileges, which render their political condition enviable to the other inhabitants of the Electorate. But, though these have invited manufacturers, and somewhat encouraged commerce, there is not wealth enough in the neighbouring country, to make such a consumption, as shall render many traders prosperous. In point of wealth, activity and address, the burgesses of Mentz are much below the opinion, which must be formed, while German cities are described and estimated by their importance in their own country, rather than by a comparison of their condition with that of others. A trader, it will be allowed, is at least as likely to appear to advantage in his business as in any other state. His intelligence may surely be, in some degree, judged of by those, who deal with him; and that we might know something of those of Mentz, we passed some of the little time we

were

were left to ourselves in endeavouring to buy trifles at their shops.

The idleness and inadvertence we generally saw are difficult to be conceived; perhaps, the trouble, experienced in purchasing a book, may give an idea of them. We wanted the German pamphlet, from which most of the above-mentioned particulars of the siege are extracted; and, as it related to a topic so general within the place, we smiled, when our friends said they would *assist* us to procure it, during a walk. Two booksellers, to whom we applied, knew nothing of it; and one supposed, that an engraved view of the works would do quite as well. Passing another shop, a young German gentleman enquired for it of the master, who was at the door, and heard, that we might have it, upon our return, in half an hour. The door, when we came back, was shut, and no knocking could procure

it

it to be opened; so that we were obliged to send into the dwelling-house. When the shopman came, he knew nothing of the book; but, being assured that his master had promised it, went away, and returned with a copy in sheets. We paid for this, and left it to be sewed, which was agreed to be done, in three hours. At that time, it was not finished, but might be had in another hour; and, after that hour, it was again promised, within two. Finally, it could not be had, that night, but would be ready in the morning, and, in the morning, it was still unfinished; we then went to Franckfort without it, and it was sent after us by a friend. This was the most aggravated instance we saw of a German trader's manners; but something like it may be almost every where met with.

From such symptoms and from the infrequency of wealth among the middle classes it is apparent, that Mentz could not have been

been important, as to commerce, even if there had been no siege, which is here mentioned as the cause of all deficiencies, and certainly is so of many. The destruction of property, occasioned by it, will not be soon remedied. The nobility have almost forsaken a place, where their palaces have been either destroyed, or ransacked; the Prince has no residence there; some of the Germans, who emigrated on account of the last siege, fled into France; the war-taxes, as well as the partial maintenance of the garrison, diminish what property remains; and all expenditure is upon a reduced footing.

The contribution of the inhabitants towards a support of the garrison is made by the very irksome means of affording them lodging. At the best houses, the doors are chalked over with the names of officers, lodged in them; which the servants dare not efface, for the soldiers must know where

to

to find their officers. In a family, whom we visited, four officers and their servants were quartered; but it must be acknowledged, that the former, so far from adding to this inconvenience by any negligent conduct, were constantly and carefully polite. We, indeed, never saw Prussian officers otherwise; and can testify, that they are as much superior to those Austrians in manners and intelligence, as they are usually said to be in military qualities.

Another obstruction, which the siege has given to the prosperity of Mentz, consists in the absence of many members of the Noble Chapter; an institution, which, however useless, or injurious to the country, occasions the expenditure of considerable sums in the capital. That of Mentz is said to be one of the richest of many similar Chapters in Germany. From such foundations the younger sons of noble families derive sometimes very ample incomes, and are but little restricted by their regulations from any enjoyment of temporal splendour. Their carriages and liveries vie with those of the other attendants at Court; they are not prohibited from wearing the ornaments of orders of knighthood; are very little enjoined to residence; are received in the environs of the Court with military honours, and allowed to reside in their separate houses. They may wear embroidery of gold, and cloths of any colours, except scarlet, or green, which, as well as silver lace, are thought too gay. Being thus permitted and enabled to become examples of luxury, their residence in any city diffuses some appearance of prosperity over it.

One of the largest buildings in Mentz is the arsenal, which fronts towards the river, and attracts the attention of those, who walk upon the quay, by having armed heads placed at the windows of the first floor, which seem to frown, with Roman sternness,

sternness, upon the passenger. In one of the principal rooms within, a party of figures in similar armour are placed at a council-board. We did not hear who contrived them; but the heads in the windows may be mistaken for real ones, at the distance of fifty yards.

The Elector of Mentz, who is chosen by a Chapter of twenty-four Canons, and is usually one of their number, is the first ecclesiastical Prince in the empire, of which he is also the Arch-chancellor and Director of the Electoral College. In the Diet, he sits on the right hand of the Emperor, affixes the seal of the Empire to its decrees, and has afterwards the custody of them among the archives. His revenues, in a time of peace, are nearly 200,000 l. annually; but, during a war, they are much less, a third part of them arising from tolls, imposed upon the navigation of the Rhine. The vineyards supply another large part; and his subjects,

subjects, not interested in them, are but little taxed, except when military preparations are to be made; the taxes are then as direct as possible, that money may be immediately collected.

The fortifications of his chief city are as much a misfortune to his country as they are an advantage to the rest of the Empire. Being always one of the first objects, on this side of the Rhine, since an enemy cannot cross the river, while so considerable a fortress and so large a garrison as it may contain, might, perhaps, check their return, the Electorate has been often the scene of a tedious warfare. From the first raising of the works by Louis the Fourteenth, their strength has never been fully tried. The surrender in 1792 was partly for the want of a proper garrison, and partly by contrivance; even in 1793, when the defence was so furious and long, the garrison, it is thought, might have held out further, if their stores had been secured in bombproof buildings. A German garrison, supported by an army, which should occupy the opposite bank of the Rhine, might be continually reinforced and supplied, so as to be conquered by nothing but the absolute demolition of the walls.

The bridge of boats over the Rhine, which, both in peace and war, is so important to the city, is now in a much better state than the French found it, being guarded, at the eastern end, by the fortifications of Cassel. Notwithstanding its great length and the rapidity of the river, it is so well constructed, as to be much less liable to injury, than might be supposed, and would probably sustain batteries, which might defeat every attempt at destroying it by fireships. It is 766 feet long, and wide enough for the passage of two carriages at once. Various repairs, and the care of a

daily

daily furvey, have continued it, fince 1661, when it was thrown over the river.

The practice of modifying the names of towns fo as to incorporate them feparately with every language, is no where more remarkable than with refpect to thofe of Germany, where a ftranger, unlefs he is aware of them, might find the variations very inconvenient. The German name for what we call Mentz, is *Maynz;* the French, which is moft ufed, *Mayence;* and the Italian *Magontio,* by defcent from the Roman *Magontiacum.* The German fynonym for Liege is *Luttich;* for Aix la Chapelle, *Achen;* for Bois le Duc, *Herzogenbufch;* and for Cologne, *Cöln,* which is pronounced *Keln.* The name borne by every town in the nation to which it belongs, fhould furely be its name, wherever it is mentioned; for the fame reafon, that words, derived into one language from another, are pronounced

nounced according to the authority of their roots, becaufe the ufe of the primary term is already eftablifhed, and there can never be a decifion between fubfequent varieties, which are cotemporary among themfelves, and are each produced by the fame arrogance of invention.

FRANCKFORT.

WE came hither by means of a paffage boat, which we were told would fhew fomething of the German populace, but which difplayed nothing fo much as the unfkilfulnefs of the German failors. Though they make this voyage, every day, they went aground in the even ftream of the Maine, and during the calmeft weather; fixing the veffel fo faft by their ill-directed ftruggle to get off, that they were compelled to bring the towing horfes to the fide and

and tug backward with the ftream. There were an hundred people in the boat; but the expedient of defiring them to remove from the part, which was aground, was never ufed. We heard, that they feldom make the voyage, without a fimilar ftoppage, not againft any fhifting fand, but upon the permanent fhelves of the river.

The diftance is about four-and-twenty miles, but we were nine hours in reaching Franckfort, the environs of which afford fome fymptoms of a commercial and opulent city, the banks of the Maine being covered for nearly the laft mile with country feats, feparated from each other by fmall pleafure grounds.

There are gates and walls to Franckfort, but the magiftrates do not opprefs travellers by a military examination at their entrance. Having feen the worthleffnefs of many places, which bear oftentatious characters either for fplendour or trade, we were furprifed prised to find in this as much of both as had been reported. The quays were well covered with goods and labourers; the streets nearest to the water are lined with shops, and those in the middle of the city with the houses of merchants, of which nearly all are spacious, and many magnificent. Some, indeed, might be called palaces, if they had nobility for their tenants; but, though the independence, which commerce spreads among the middle classes, does not entirely deter the German nobility from a residence here, the finest houses are the property of merchants.

In our way to the *Cigne Blanc*, which is one of the best inns, we passed many of so good an appearance, that it was difficult to believe there could be better in a German city. But Franckfort, which is the pride of Germany, in this respect, has probably a greater number of large inns than any other place of equal extent in Europe. The fairs

fill

fill thefe, twice in a year, for three weeks, at each time; and the order, which is indifpenfible then, continues at other periods, to the furprife and comfort of ftrangers.

This city has been juftly defcribed by many travellers; and Doctor MOORE has treated of its inhabitants with the eafe and elegant animation of his peculiar manner. We fhall not affume the difadvantage of entering upon the fame fubject after him. The inhabitants of Franckfort are very diftinct, as to manners and information, from the other Germans; but they are fo far like to thofe of our own commercial cities, that one able account leaves fcarcely any thing new to be feen, or told, concerning them.

All their bleffings of liberty, intelligence, and wealth are obferved with the more attention, becaufe they cannot be approached, except through countries afflicted by arbitrary power, ignorance and poverty. The
exiftence

GERMANY. 395

existence of such a city, in such a situation, is little less than a *phenomenon*; the causes of which are so various and minute as to make the effect, at first sight, appear almost accidental. The jealousy of the neighbouring Princes towards each other, is the known, and, certainly, the chief cause of its exterior protection against each; the continuance of its interior liberties is probably owing to the circumstance, which, but for that jealousy, would expose it to subjection from without,—the smallness of its territory. Where the departments of government must be very few, very difficult to be rendered expensive to the public, and very near to their inspection, the ambition of individuals can be but little tempted to contrive encroachments upon the community. So complexly are the chief causes of its exterior and interior independence connected with each other.

As to the first of these, it may, perhaps, be

be replied, that a similar jealousy has not always been sufficient to protect similar cities; and Dantzick is the recent instance of its insufficiency. But the jealousy, as to Dantzick, though similar, was not equal to this, and the temptation to oppose it was considerably greater. What would the most capable of the neighbouring Princes gain by the seizure of Franckfort? A place of strength? No. A place capable of paying taxes? Yes; but taxes, which would be re-imposed upon commodities, consumed partly by his own subjects, whose property is his own already, and partly by those of his neighbours, to whose jealousy they would afford an additional and an unappeasable provocation. Dantzick, on the contrary, being a seaport, was, if not strong, capable of supplying strength, and might pay taxes, which should not fall entirely upon its neighbours, but upon the distant countries, that traffick with it. And even to to these confiderations it is unneceffary to refort, unlefs we can fuppofe, that defpotifm would have no effect upon commerce; a fuppofition which does not require to be refuted. If a fevere taxation was introduced here, and, in fo fmall a diftrict, taxation muft be fevere to be productive; if fuch a taxation was to be introduced, and if the other advantage of conqueft, that of a forcible levy of foldiers, was attempted, commerce would vanifh in filence before the oppreffor, and the Prince, that fhould feize the liberties of Franckfort, would find nothing but thofe liberties in his grafp.

On the other hand, what are the advantages of permitting the independence of fuch a city to the fovereigns, who have the power of violating it? Thofe of a neutral barrier are well known, but apply only to military, or political circumftances. The others are the market, which Franckfort affords, for the produce and manufactures

of

of all the neighbouring ſtates; its value as a banking *depôt* and *emporium*, in which Princes may place their money, without rendering it liable to the orders of each other, or from which they may derive loans, by negotiating ſolely and directly with the lenders; its incapacity for offenſive meaſures; and its uſefulneſs as a place of meeting to themſelves, or their miniſters, when political connections are to be diſcuſſed.

That the inhabitants do enjoy this independence without and freedom within, we believe, not becauſe they are aſſerted by treaties, or political forms; of which the former might not have ſurvived the temporary intereſts, that concluded them, and the latter might be ſubdued by corruption, if there were the means of it; but becauſe they were acknowledged to us by many temperate and diſcerning perſons, as much aloof from faction, as they were from the affectation,

affectation, or servility, that sometimes makes men boast themselves free, only because they have, or would be thought to have, a little share in oppressing others. Many such persons declared to us, that they had a substantial, practical freedom; and we thought a testimony to their actual enjoyments more valuable than any formal acknowledgments of their rights. As to these latter securities, indeed, Franckfort is no better provided than other imperial cities, which have proved their inutility. It stands in the same list with Cologne, but is as superior to it in government as in wealth.

The inhabitants having had the good sense to foresee, that fortifications might render them a more desirable prize to their neighbours, at the same time that their real protection must depend upon other means, have done little more than sustain their antient walls, which are sufficient to defend them against a surprise by small parties.

They

They maintain no troops, except a few companies of city-guards, and make their contributions to the army of the Empire in specie. These companies are filled chiefly with middle-aged men, whose appearance bespeaks the plenty and peacefulness of the city. Their uniforms, blue and white, are of the cut of those in the prints of MARLBOROUGH's days; and their grenadiers' caps are of the same peaked sort, with tin facings, impressed with the city arms.

In wars with France, the fate of Franckfort has usually depended upon that of Mentz, which is properly called the key of Germany, on the western frontier. In the campaign of 1792, Custine detached 3000 troops of the 11,000, with which he had besieged Mentz, and these reached Franckfort, early in the morning of the 22d of October. NEUWINGER, their commander, sent a letter to the magistrates from Custine, demanding a contribution of two millions

of

of florins, which, by a negotiation at Mentz, was reduced to a million and a half, for the prefent. Notice was accordingly given in the city, that the magiftrates would receive money at four per cent. intereft, and, on the 23d, at break of day, it began to flow in to the Council-houfe from all quarters. Part was immediately given to NEUWIN-GER, but payment of the reft was delayed; fo that Cuftine came himfelf on the 27th, and, by throwing the hoftages into prifon, obtained, on the 31ft of October, the remainder of the firft million. For the fecond, the magiftrates gave fecurity to NEUWIN-GER, but it was never paid; the Convention difavowed great part of the proceedings of Cuftine, and the money was not again demanded.

The French, during the whole of their ftay, were very eager to fpread exaggerated accounts of their numbers. Troops were accordingly marched out at one gate of the city,

city, with very little parade, that they might enter with much pomp and in a longer column, at the other. The inhabitants, who were not expert at military numeration, easily believed, that the first party had joined other troops, and that the whole amounted to treble their real number. After the entry of the Prussians, this contrivance was related by prisoners.

The number of troops, left in the city by Custine, on his retirement from the neighbouring posts, in the latter end of November, was 1800 men, with two pieces of cannon. On the 28th, when the Prussian Lieutenant Pellet brought a summons to surrender, Helden, the commander, having sent to Custine for reinforcements and cannon, was answered, that no men could be spared; and that, as to cannon, he might use the city artillery. Helden endeavoured to remove this from the arsenal; but the populace, encouraged by the neighbourhood

neighbourhood of the Pruffians, rofe to prevent him; and there might have been a confiderable tumult, if Cuftine had not arrived, on the 29th, and affured the magiftrates, that the garrifon fhould retire, rather than expofe the place to a fiege. The city then became tranquil, and remained fo till the 2d of December, when the inhabitants, being in church, firft knew by the noife of cannon, that the place was attacked.

General Helden would then have taken his two cannon to the gate, which was contended for, but the inhabitants, remembering Cuftine's promife, would permit no refiftance; they cut the harnefs of the horfes, broke the cannon wheels, and themfelves opened the gates to the Pruffians, or rather to the Heffians; for the advanced corps of the affailants was chiefly formed of them. About 100 fell in this attack. Of the French 41 were killed; 139 wounded; and 800 taken prifoners. The remainder of the

1800 reached Cuſtine's army. A monument, erected without the northern gate of the city, commemorates the loſs of the 100 aſſailants, on the ſpot, on which they fell. Thus Franckfort, having happily but few fortifications, was loſt and regained, without a ſiege; while Mentz, in a period of ſix more months, had nearly all its beſt buildings deſtroyed, by a ſimilar change of maſters.

We ſtayed here almoſt a week, which was well occupied by viſits, but ſhewed nothing in addition to what is already known of the ſociety of the place. Manners, cuſtoms, the topics of converſation and even dreſs, differ very ſlightly from thoſe of London, in ſimilar ranks; the merchants of Franckfort have more generally the advantages of travel, than thoſe of England, but they have not that minute knowledge of modern events and characters, which an attention to public tranſactions renders

common

common in our island. Those, who have been in England, or who speak English, seem desirous to discuss the state of parliamentary transactions and interests, and to remedy the thinness of their own public topics, by introducing ours. In such discussions one error is very general from their want of experience. The faculty of making a speech is taken for the standard of intellectual power in every sort of exertion; though there is nothing better known in countries, where public speakers are numerous enough to be often observed, than that persons may be educated to oratory, so as to have a facility, elegance and force in it, distinct from the endowments of deliberative wisdom; may be taught to speak in terms remote from common use, to combine them with an unfailing dexterity of arrangement, and to invest every thought with its portion of artificial dignity, who,

, through

through the chaos of benefits and evils, which the agitation of difficult times throws up before the eye of the politician, shall be able to see no gleam of light, to describe no direct path, to discern no difference between greater and lesser evils, nor to think one wholesome truth for a confiding and an honest country. To estimate the general intellectual powers of men, tutored to oratory, from their success in the practice of it, is as absurd as to judge of corporeal strength from that of one arm, which may have been rendered unusually strong by exercise and art.

Of the society at Franckfort, Messrs. Bethman, the chief bankers, seem able to collect a valuable part; and their politeness to strangers induces them to do it often. A traveller, who misses their table, loses, both as to conversation and elegant hospitality, a welcome proof of what freedom and commerce can do against the mental and physical desolation otherwise spread over the country.

The assistance, which the mutual use of languages gives to a connection between distant places, we were happy to see existing and increasing, to the advantage of England, at Franckfort. At the Messrs. Bethmans', one day, French was nearly excluded, the majority being able to converse with nine or ten English, who were there, in their own language. Of the merchants, who have not been in England, several speak English, without difficulty, and the rising generation, it is said, will be generally accomplished in it.

One of the luxuries of Franckfort is a *Cabinet Literaire*, which is open to strangers by the introduction of members. There the best periodical publications of the Continent are received, and their titles immediately entered in a book, so that the reading is not disturbed by conversation with the librarian. It excited our shame to hear, that some contrivance had, for several months, prevented the society from receiving a very valuable English publication.

After this, the Theatre may seem to require some notice. It is a modern, but not an elegant building, standing in an area, that renders it convenient of access, and nearly in the middle of the city. The interior, which has been gaudily decorated, contains a pit, three rows of boxes, that surround the audience part, and a gallery over them in the centre. It is larger than the Little Theatre in the Haymarket, and, in form, resembles that of Covent Garden, except that six or seven of the central boxes, in each tier, encroach upon the oval figure by a projection over the pit. The boxes are let by the year; the price of admission for non-subscribers, is a florin, for which they may find places in the boxes, engaged by by their friends, or in the pit, which is in the same proportion of esteem as that at an Opera-house.

The performances are plays and operas alternately; both in German; and the music of the latter chiefly by German composers. The players are very far beneath mediocrity; but the orchestra, when we heard it, accorded with the fame of German musicians, for spirit and precision. In these qualities even the wandering parties, that play at inns, are very seldom deficient.

The stage was well lighted, but the other parts of the theatre were left in duskiness, which scarcely permitted us to see the diamonds, profusely worn by several ladies. Six o'clock is the hour of beginning, and the performances conclude soon after nine.

The Cabinet Literaire and the Theatre are the only permanent places of public amusement at Franckfort, which is, however, in want of no more, the inhabitants being accustomed to pass much of their time in friendly parties, at their houses. Though wealth is, of course, earnestly and universally sought for in a place purely mercantile, we were assured, that the richest persons, and there are some, who have above half a million sterling, find no more attention in these parties than others. This was acknowledged and separately boasted of by some of the very rich, and by those who were comparatively poor. We are so far able to report it for true, as that we could never discern the least traces of the officiousness, or subserviency that, in a corrupt and debased state of society, frequently point to the wealthiest individuals in every private party.

These and many other circumstances would probably render Franckfort a place of residence for foreigners, if the magistrates, either dreading the increase of luxury, or the interference of strangers with their

GERMANY.

their commerce, did not prevent this by prohibiting them from being lodged otherwise than at inns. It was with difficulty, that an English officer, acting as Commissary to some of the German regiments, lately raised upon our pay, could obtain an exemption from this rule, at the request of the Hanoverian Minister.

Round the city, are several well-disposed walks, as pleasant as the flatness of the nearer country will permit; and, at intervals, along these, are the country houses of the merchants, who do not choose to go beyond the city territories, for a residence. Saxenhausen, a small town, on the other side of the Maine, though incorporated with Franckfort, as to jurisdiction, and connected with it by a bridge, is chiefly inhabited by watermen and other labourers.

We left Franckfort, after a stay of six days, fortified by a German passport from M. de Swartzhoff, the Hanoverian Minister, who

who obligingly adviſed us to be prepared with one in the native language of the Auſtrian officers. At Mentz, the ceremonies of examination were rendered much more troubleſome than before, the Governor, General Kalkreuth, happening to be in the great ſquare, who choſe to make ſeveral travellers wait as if for a ſort of review before him, though, after all, nothing was to be ſaid but "Go to the Commandant, who will look at your paſſports." This Commandant was M. de Lucadou, a gentleman of conſiderate and polite manners, who, knowing our friends in Mentz, added to his confirmation of M. de Swartzhoff's paſſport an addreſs to M. de Wilde, the Intendant of ſome ſalt mines in Switzerland, which he recommended to us to ſee. Theſe circumſtances are neceſſary to be mentioned here, becauſe they ſoon led to a diſagreeable and very contradictory event in our journey.

The

The next morning, we set out from Mentz, and were conducted by our voiturier over a summer road, on the left bank of the Rhine, then flowing with the melted snows of Switzerland.

OPPENHEIM.

THIS is the first town of the Palatinate, on arriving from the north; and it bears marks of the devastation, inflicted upon that country, in the last century, more flagrant than could be expected, when the length of the intervening time, and the complete recovery of other cities from similar disasters, are considered. Louis the Fourteenth's fury has converted it from a populous city into little more than a picturesque ruin. It was burned in 1668; and the walls, which remain in double, or sometimes in treble circles, are more visible, at a distance, a distance, than the streets, which have been thinly erected within them. Above all, is the *Landscroon*, or crown of the country, a castle erected on an eminence, which commands the Rhine, and dignifies the view from it, for several miles. The whole city, or rather ruin, stands on a brow, over this majestic river.

The gates do not now open directly into streets, but into lanes of stone walls between vineyards and gardens, formed on the site of houses, never restored, since the fire. The town itself has shrunk from its antient limits into a few streets in the centre. In some of the interstices, corn grows up to the walls of the present houses. In others the ruins of former buildings remain, which the owners have not been tempted to remove, for the sake of cultivating their sites. Of the cathedral, said to have been once the finest on the Rhine, nearly all the walls and the tower still exist; but these are the only

only remains of grandeur in a city, which seems entirely incapable of overcoming in this century the wretchedness it inherits from the last.

Had the walls been as strong as they are extensive, this place might not improbably have endured a siege in the present age, having been several times lost and regained. It was surrendered to the French, without a contest, in the campaign of 1792. After their retreat from Worms, and during the siege of Mentz, it was occupied by the Prussians; and, in December 1793, when the allies retired from Alsace, the Duke of Brunswick established his head-quarters in it, for the purpose of covering the fortress. His army ovens remained near the northern gate, in July 1794, when we passed through it. In October of the same year it fell again into the hands of the French.

No city on the banks of the Rhine is so well seated for affording a view of it as this, which,

which, to the north, overlooks all its windings as far as Mentz, and, southward, commands them towards Worms. The river is also here of a noble breadth and force, beating so vehemently against the water-mills, moored near the side, that they seem likely to be borne away with the current. A city might be built on the site of Oppenheim, which should faintly rival the castle of Goodesberg, in the richness, though not in the sublimity of its prospect.

From hence the road leads through a fertile country of corn and vines, but at a greater distance from the river, to Worms, five or six miles from which it becomes broad, straight, and bordered with regularly-planted trees, that form an avenue to the city. Soon after leaving Oppenheim, we had the first symptom of an approach to the immediate theatre of the war, meeting a waggon, loaded with wounded soldiers. On this road, there was a long train of carriages,

riages, taking stores to some military *depôt*. The defacement of the Elector's arms, on posts near the road, shewed also, that the country had been lately occupied by the French; as the delay in cutting the ripe corn did, that there was little expectation of their return.

WORMS.

THE condition of Worms is an aggravated repetition of the wretchedness of Oppenheim. It suffered something in the war, which the unfortunate Elector, son-in-law of our James the First, provoked by accepting the kingdom of Bohemia. Louis the Fourteenth came upon it next, and, in 1669, burned every thing that could be consumed. Nothing was restored, but on that part, which was the centre of the antient city; and the walls include, as at Oppenheim,

Oppenheim, corn and vineyards upon the ground, which was once covered with houses, and which plainly appears to have been so, from the lanes that pass between, and doors that open into the inclosures. A much larger space is so covered, than at Oppenheim, for you are some time in driving from the northern gate of the old city to the first street of the present one.

On the right of the road stands the skeleton of the Electoral palace, which the French burned in one of the late campaigns; and it is as curious as melancholy to observe how the signs of antient and modern desolation mingle with each other. On one hand is a palace, burned by the present French; on the other, the walls of a church, laid open by Louis the Fourteenth.

The first and principal street of the place leads through these mingled ruins, and through rows of dirty houses, miserably tenanted,

tenanted, to the other end of the city. A few others branch from it, chiefly towards the Rhine, including sometimes the ruins, and sometimes the repaired parts of churches; of which streets, narrow, ill-paved and gloomy, consists the city of Worms. The French General, that lately wrote to Paris, "We entered the fair episcopal city of Worms," may be supposed to have derived his terms from a geographical dictionary, rather than from a view of his conquest.

We were now in a place, occupied by part of the acting army of the allies, which, if not immediately liable to be attacked, was to be defended by the maintenance of posts, at a very short distance. Troops passed through it daily, for the service of these posts. The noise of every cannonade was audible, and the result of every engagement was immediately known, for it might make an advance, or a retreat necessary from Worms. The wounded men arrived, soon after the intelligence, to the military hospitals of the Prussians. A city, so circumstanced, seemed to differ but little from a camp; and we were aware, for a few hours, of a departure from the security and order of civil life.

The inn, which was not otherwise a mean building, was nearly destitute of furniture; so that the owner was prepared to receive any sort of guests, or masters. The only provision which we could obtain was bread, the commonest sort of wine, and one piece of cold veal; for the city was under military jurisdiction, and no guests were allowed to have more than one dish at their table.

In the afternoon, we saw, for the first time, a crowd in a German city. A narrow waggon, of which nearly all but the wheels was basket-work, had arrived from the army, with a wounded officer, who lay upon the

floor,

floor, supported by his servant, but occasionally rose to return the salutes of passengers. This was the Prince of Anhalt Plessis, who had been wounded, in the morning, when the French attacked all the neighbouring lines of the allies, and an indecisive engagement ensued, the noise of which had been distinctly heard, at Worms. He was hurt in the leg, and descended, with much difficulty, from the waggon; but did not, for an instant, lose the elegance of his address, and continued bowing through the passage to his apartment. No doubt was entertained of his recovery, but there seemed to be a considerable degree of sympathy, attending this young man.

We had not time to look into the churches, or numerous monasteries, that yet remain, at Worms; the war appeared to have depopulated the latter, for not a monk was to be seen. The cathedral, or church of St. Mary and St. Peter, is one of the moft antient facred buildings in Germany, having been founded at leaft as early as the commencement of the feventh century. One of the prebends was eftablifhed in 1033, another in 1058. The Dominicans, Carmelites, Capuchins and Auguftines have each a monaftery, at Worms; as have the Ciftercians and the Auguftines a nunnery. A Proteftant church was alfo confecrated, on the 9th of June 1744; fomething more than two hundred years, after the ineffectual conference held here of Proteftant and Catholic divines, which Charles the Fifth interrupted, when Melancthon, on one fide, and Echius, on the other, had engaged in it, ordering them to refume their arguments, in his prefence, at Ratifbon. This meeting was five years previous to the celebrated diet of Worms, at which Charles, having then eftimated the temporal ftrength of the two parties, openly fhewed his animofity to the Proteftants, as Maurice

of

of Saxony did his intriguing ambition, by referring the queftion to the Council of Trent.

The Jews, at Worms, inhabit a feparate ftreet, and have a fynagogue, of great antiquity, their numbers having been once fuch as to endanger the peace of the city; but, in 1689, when the French turned their fynagogue into a ftable, they fled with the reft of the opulent inhabitants to Holland. Thofe of the prefent day can have very few articles of traffic, except money, the changing of which may have been frequent, on account of the neighbourhood of France.

Worms is fomewhat connected with Englifh hiftory, having been occupied by the troops, which James the Firft ufelefsly fent to the affiftance of the profcribed Elector Palatine, when his juft abhorrence of continental wars was once, though tardily, overcome by the entreaties of his daughter. Here too George the Second held his head-quarters,

quarters, from the 7th to the 20th of September 1743; on the 14th of which month, Lord Carteret concluded, in his name, an offenſive and defenſive treaty with the Miniſters of Hungary and Sardinia.

This city, like Cologne, retains ſome affectation of the Roman form of government, to which it was rendered ſubject by Cæſar, with the title of *Auguſta Vangionum*. The STADTMEISTER is ſometimes called the CONSUL, and the SCHULTHEIS, or Mayor, the PRÆTOR. But, in 1703, ſome trivial tumult afforded a pretence for aboliſhing its little remains of liberty, and the Elector Palatine was declared its protector. This blow completed the deſolation, which the diſaſters of the preceding century had commenced; and a city, that was once called the market of the Palatinate, as the Palatinate was reputed the market of Germany, continues to exhibit nothing more than the ruins of its antient proſperity.

Few

GERMANY.

Few of the present inhabitants can be the descendants of those, who witnessed its destruction in 1689; for we could not find, that the particulars of that event were much known, or commemorated by them, dreadful and impressive as they must have been. A column of Louis the Fourteenth's army had entered the city, in September of the preceding year, under the command of the Marquis de Bonfleur, who soon distressed the inhabitants by preparations for blowing up the walls with gunpowder. The mines were so numerous and large, as to threaten nothing less than the entire overwhelming of the city; but, being fired at different times, the walls of the houses were left standing, though they shook with almost every explosion. The artillery and balls had been previously carried away to Landau, or Mentz, then possessed by Louis. At length, on the 12th of May 1689, the

Intendant

Intendant sent the melancholy news to the magistracy, that he had received orders from his monarch to burn the whole city. Six days were allowed for the departure of the inhabitants and the removal of their property; which period was prolonged by their entreaties to nineteen. At the expiration of these, on Ascension Day, the 31st of May, the French grenadiers were employed from twelve o'clock, till four, in placing combustibles about the houses and public buildings, against several of which large heaps of hay and straw were raised. The word being then given, fire was set to almost every house at once, and, in a few hours, the city was reduced to ashes; the conflagration being so general and strong as to be visible in day-light at the distance of more than thirty English miles. Such was one of the calamities of a city, so unfortunately situated, that the chapter of the cathedral

cathedral alone proved a lofs by wars, previous to the year 1743, amounting to 1,262,749 florins.

The attention, due to fo memorable a place, detained us at Worms, till the voiturier talked of being unable to reach Manheim, before the gates would be fhut, and we let him drive vehemently towards

FRANCKENTHAL,

ANOTHER place, deftroyed by Louis the Fourteenth, but reftored upon a plan fo uniform and convenient, that nothing but a fuller population is neceffary to confirm its title of a flourifhing city. The ftreets, which interfect each other at right angles, are wide and exactly ftraight; the houfes are handfomely built, but the poverty or indolence of the owners fuffers them to partake of the air of neglect, which is general

in

in German habitations; and the streets, though spacious and not ill-paved, had so few passengers, that the depopulation of the place seemed to be rendered the more observable by its grandeur.

Yet it would be unfair to estimate the general prosperity of Franckenthal by its present circumstances, even had we stayed long enough to know them more accurately. This place had been occupied but a few weeks before by the French army, who had plundered it, as well as several other towns of the Palatinate, after the retreat of the allies from Alsace, at the latter end of 1793. The inhabitants had, for the most part, returned to their houses; but their commerce, which is said to have been not contemptible, could not be so easily restored. The manufactures of porcelain, cloths, silks, spangles, vinegar and soap, of which some were established and all are protected by the wise liberality of the Elector, though far

from

GERMANY. 429

from being anfwerable, either in their capitals, or produce, to the Englifh idea of fimilar enterprifes, command fome fhare with England and France in fupplying the reft of Germany. One method of facilitating the operations of trade the Elector has advantageoufly adopted here; that of inftituting a court upon the fpot for the decifion of all caufes, in which the traders are interefted; and at his expence a navigable canal has been formed from the town to the Rhine. Artifts and merchants have alfo fome privileges, at Franckenthal, of which that of being exempt from the military prefs is not the leaft.

This prefs, or levy, is the method, by which all the German Princes return their contingents to the army of the Empire. The population of every town and diftrict in their dominions is known with fufficient accuracy, and a fettled number of recruits is fupplied by each. When thefe are wanted,

notice

notice is given, that the men of a certain age muſt aſſemble and caſt lots for the ſervice. Thoſe, who are drawn, may find ſubſtitutes, but with this condition, that the deputy muſt be at leaſt as tall as his principal; a regulation, which makes the price of ſubſtitutes depend upon their height, and frequently renders it impoſſible for the principals to avail themſelves of the permiſſion. A farmer in this neighbourhood, who was conſiderably above ſix feet in height, could not obtain a ſubſtitute for leſs than a hundred louis d'ors.

Another unpleaſant condition is attached to this exchange: if the ſubſtitute is diſabled, or deſerts, another muſt be ſupplied; and, if he carries his arm or accoutrements away, theſe muſt be paid for by the perſon, who ſent him.

After a ride of a few miles, we reached

OGGER-

OGGERSHEIM,

A SMALL town, on the weſt bank of the Rhine, rebuilt in uniform ſtreets, like Franckenthal, having been deſtroyed by the ſame exertion of Louis the Fourteenth's cruelty. Here alſo the modern French had very lately been, and ſome of the ruins, left near the road by Louis, appeared to have ſerved them for kitchens in their excurſion.

At the eaſt end of the town, towards the Rhine, ſtands a chateau of the Elector, built with modern, but not very admirable taſte, and commanding the diſtant river in ſeveral fine points of view. We could not be admitted to ſee the inſide, which is ſaid to have been ſplendidly decorated; for the French had juſt diſmantled it of the furniture.

The road from hence to Manheim was bordered

bordered for its whole length, of at leaſt two miles, by rows of poplars, of which ſome ſtill remain near Oggerſheim ; but thoſe within a mile and a half of Manheim have been felled at one or two feet from the ground. This was done in December 1793, when the French began to advance from Landau, and were expected to beſiege Manheim, their operations againſt which might have been covered, in ſome meaſure, by this noble alley.

Near the Rhine, the road is now commanded by two forts, of which one was thrown up during the approach of the French, and completed in the middle of the ſummer, with great care. Theſe contribute much to the preſent ſecurity of the city, which might otherwiſe be bombarded from the oppoſite bank of the river, even by an enemy, who ſhould not be able and ſhould not propoſe to attempt the conqueſt of the place. They are ditched and pal-
liſadoed,

lifadoed, but, being divided from the body of the city, by the Rhine, are, of courfe, without the communication, which renders fuch works capable of a long defence. Round one of thefe forts, the road now winds, entering a part of the works, near the bridge, where there is a guardhoufe for the troops of the Elector.

MANHEIM.

IT was twilight, when we approached Manheim; and the palace, the numerous turrets and the fortifications had their grandeur probably increafed by the obfcurity. The bridge of boats is not fo long as that at Mentz; but we had time enough in paffing it to obferve the extent of the city, on the left of which the Neckar pours itfelf into the Rhine, fo that two fides are entirely wafhed by their ftreams. At the next guard-houfe, where we were detained by the ufual enquiries, the troops were more numerous; and furely no military figures ever accorded fo well with the gloomy gates, and walls they guarded. The uniform of the Palatine light troops is a clofe jacket of motley brown, and pantaloons of the fame that reach to their half-boots. They have black helmets, with crefts and fronts of brafs, large whifkers, and their faces, by conftant expofure to the fun, are of the deepeft brown that can be, without approaching to black. As they ftood fingly on the ramparts, or in groups at the gates, their bronze faces and Roman helmets feemed of a deeper hue, than the gloom, that partly concealed their figures.

The entrance into Manheim, from the Rhine, is by a fpacious ftreet, which leads directly into the centre of the city, and to a large fquare, planted with limes, confifting, on one fide, of public buildings, and,

on

on the other, of several noble houses, one of which is the chief inn, called the *Cour Palatine*. This is the first city in Germany, that can answer, by its appearance, the expectations of a foreigner, who has formed them from books. Its aspect is truly that of a capital and of the residence of a Court; except that in the day-time a traveller may be somewhat surprised at the fewness of passengers and the small shew of traffic, amidst such public buildings, and in streets of such convenience and extent. The fairness, the grandeur and the statelines, which he may have seen attributed to other German cities, till he is as much disgusted as deceived by every idea derived from description, may be perceived in several parts of Manheim, and the justness of disposition in all.

Nor is the beauty of the present city solely owing to the destruction of the antient one by Louis the Fourteenth, in 1689, the year of general devastation in the Palatinate. It was laid out in right lines, though to a lefs extent, in the beginning of the feventeenth century, when Frederic the Fifth laid the foundation of the fortifications, behind which a town was built, that adopted the antient name of Manheim, from a neighbouring one then in decay. Thefe were the fortifications and the town deftroyed by the French in 1689. The plan of both was but extended, when the prefent works were formed upon the fyftem of Cohorn, and the city by degrees reftored, with ftreets, which, interfecting each other at right angles, divide it into an hundred and feven fquare portions. The number of the inhabitants, exclufive of the garrifon, was, in 1784, 21,858.

Some of the ftreets are planted with rows of trees; and there are five or fix open places, fuitable for promenades, or markets. The cuftomhoufe, which forms a fide to

one

one of thefe, is a noble ftone building, rather appearing to be a palace, than an office, except that under the colonnades, which furround it, are fhops for jewellery and other commodities.

The Electoral palace, which opens, on one fide, to the city, and, on the other, to the ramparts, was built by the Elector Charles-Philippe, who, in the year 1721, removed his refidence hither from Heidelberg, on account of fome difference with the magiftrates, or, as is faid, of the prevalence of religious difputes in that city. He began to erect it in 1720; but the edifice was not completed, till the right wing was added by the prefent Elector, not to be ufed as a refidence, but to contain a gallery of paintings, cabinets of antiquities and natural hiftory, a library, treafury and *manege*. We paffed a morning in viewing the apartments in the other wing, all the paintings and books having been removed from this, as well as great part of the furniture from the whole palace, in the dread of an approaching bombardment. The person, who shewed them, took care to keep the credit of each room safe, by assuring us at the door, that it was not in its usual condition. The Elector had been, for some months, at Munich, but the Duke and Duchess of Deux Ponts and their family have resided in this palace, since their retirement from Deux Ponts, in the latter end of the campaign of 1792.

The rooms are all lofty, and floored with inlaid work of oak and chesnut; the ceilings, for the most part, painted; and the walls covered with tapestry, finely wrought, both as to colour and design. Some of this came from a manufactory, established by the Elector, at Franckenthal.

The furniture, left in several of the rooms, was grand and antient, but could never have been so costly as those, who have

have seen the mansions of wealthy individuals in England, would expect to find in a palace. The Elector's state-bed was inclosed not only by a railing, but by a glass case to the height of the ceiling, with windows, that could be opened at pleasure, to permit a conversation with his courtiers, when compliments were paid literally at a levee. In the court of France, this practice continued even to very late years, and there were three distinct privileges of entrée, denoting the time, at which persons of different classes were permitted to enter the chamber. In the Earl of Portland's embassy for King William to Louis the Fourteenth, it was thought a signal mark of honour, that he was admitted to his audience, not only in the chamber, but within the rails; and there the French Monarch stood with the three young Princes, his grandsons, the Count de Tholouse, the Duke d'Aumont and the Mareschal de Noailles.

The Duke made his speech covered, after which the King entered into converfation with him, for feveral minutes.

One room, at Manheim, was called the Silver Chamber, from the quantity of folid filver, ufed about the furniture. Such articles as could be carried away entire, had been removed, but the walls were disfigured by the lofs of the ornaments torn from them, on account of their value. In feveral rooms, the furniture, that remained, was partly packed, to be carried away upon the next alarm. The contents of the wardrobe were in this ftate, and the interior of thefe now defolated apartments feemed like the fkeleton of grandeur. The beauty of the painted ceilings, however, the richnefs of the various profpects, commanded by the windows, and the great extent of the building fufficiently accounted for the reputation, which this palace has, of being the fineft in Germany.

It is built of stone, which has somewhat the reddish hue of that used at Mentz, and, though several parts are positively disapproved by persons of skill in architecture, the whole is certainly a grand and sumptuous building.

The situation of Manheim and the scenery around it are viewed to great advantage from the tower of the Observatory, in which strangers are politely received by the Professor of Astronomy, whose residence is established in it. From this are seen the fruitful plains of the Palatinate, spreading, on all sides, to bold mountains, of which those of Lorrain, that extend on the west, lose in distance the variety of their colouring, and, assuming a blue tint, retain only the dignity of their form. Among these, the vast and round headland, called the *Tonnesberg*, which is in sight, during the greatest part of the journey from Mentz to Manheim, is pre-eminent.

But

But the chain, that binds the horizon on the east, and is known by the name of the *Bergstrasse*, or road of mountains, is near enough to display all their wild irregularity of shape; the forest glens, to which they open, and the various tints of rock and soil, of red and purple, that mingle with the corn and wood on their lower steeps. These mountains are seen in the north from their commencement near Franckfort, and this line is never interrupted from thence southward into Switzerland. The rivals to them, on the south west, are the mountains of Alsace, which extend in long perspective, and at a distance appear to unite with those of the Bergstrasse. Among the numerous towns and villages that throng the Palatinate, the spires of Oppenheim and Worms are distinctly visible to the north; almost beneath the eye are those of Franckenthal, and Oggersheim, and to the southward Spires shews its many towers."

In the nearer scene the Neckar, after tumbling from among the forests of the Bergstrasse, falls into the Rhine, a little below the walls of Manheim; and the gardens of a summer chateau belonging to the Elector occupy the angle between the two rivers.

These gardens were now surrendered by the Prince to be the camp of three thousand of his troops, detached from the garrison of the city, which, at this time, consisted of nearly ten thousand men. In several places, on the banks of the two rivers, batteries were thrown up, and, near the camp, a regular fort, for the purpose of commanding both; so that Manheim, by its natural and artificial means of defence, was supposed to be rendered nearly unassailable, on two sides. On that of Heidelberg, it was not so, secure; nor could the others be defended by a garrison of less than 15,000 men. It was on this account, that the Elector detained

ten

ten thousand of his troops from actual service, contrary, as is said, to the remonstrances of the Emperor, who offered, but without success, to garrison his capital with Austrians. From the observatory, the camp and the works were easily seen, and, by the help of a Dollond telescope, the only optical instrument remaining, the order of both was so exactly pointed out by our guide, that it was not difficult to comprehend the uses of them. Military preparations, indeed, occurred very frequently in Manheim. In the gardens of the chief Electoral palace, extending to the ramparts over the Rhine, cannon were planted; which were as regularly guarded by sentinels as in the other parts of the fortifications.

All the gates of Manheim appear to be defended by fortifications of unusual strength. Besides two broad ditches, there are batteries, which play directly upon the bridges, and might destroy them in a few minutes.
The

The gates are guarded, with the utmost strictness, and no person is suffered to enter them, after ten at night, without the express permission of the governor. When a courier arrives, who wishes to use his privilege of passing, at all hours, he puts some token of his office into a small tin box, which is kept on the outside of the ditch, to be drawn across it by a cord, that runs upon a roller on each bank. The officer of the guard carries this to the governor, and obtains the keys; but so much time is passed in this sort of application, that couriers, when the nights are short, usually wait the opening of the gates, which is soon after day-light, in summer, and at six, or seven, in winter.

The absence of the Elector, we were assured, had much altered the appearance of Manheim, where scarcely a carriage was now to be seen, though there were traces enough of the gaiety and general splendour

of

of this little Court. Here are an Opera Houfe, a German Comedy, an Amateur Concert, an Electoral Lottery, an Academy of Sculpture and Defign, and an Academy of Sciences. The Opera performances are held in a wing of the palace, and were eftablifhed in 1742, but have not attained much celebrity, being fupported chiefly by performers from the other Theatre. This laft is called a national eftablifhment, the players being Germans, and the Theatre founded in 1779 at the expence of the Elector. The Baron de Dahlberg, one of his Minifters, has the fuperintendance of it. The Amateur Concert is held, every Friday, during the winter, and is much frequented.

The Electoral Lotteries, for there are two, are drawn in the prefence of the Minifter of Finances, and one of them is lefs difadvantageous for the gamefters than is ufual with fuch undertakings. That, which

consists

consists of chances determined in the customary way, gives the Elector an advantage of only five to four over the subscribers. The other, which is formed upon the more intricate model of that of Genoa, entitles the subscribers to prizes, proportioned to the number of times a certain ticket issues from the wheel, five numbers being drawn out of ninety; or rather five drawings of one number each being successively made out of ninety tickets. A ticket, which issues once in these five drawings, wins fifteen times the value of the stake; one, that should be drawn each of the five times, would entitle the owner to have his original stake multiplied by sixty thousand, and the product would be his prize. The undertaker of this latter Lottery has the chances immensely in his favour.

From the very large income, to which these Lotteries contribute a part, the present Elector has certainly made considerable disburfements,

burfements, with ufeful purpofes, if not to ufeful effects. Of his foundation are the Academy of Sciences, which was opened in 1763, for weekly fittings, and has proceeded to fome correfpondence with other Academies; the German Society, eftablifhed for the eafy purpofe of purifying and the difficult one of fixing language; the Cabinet of Phyfics, or rather of experimental philofophy, celebrated for the variety and magnitude of its inftruments, among which are two burning glaffes of three feet diameter, faid to be capable of liquefying bodies, even bottles filled with water, at 10 feet diftance; the Obfervatory, of 108 feet high, in which all the chief inftruments were Englifh; a Botanical Garden and Directorfhip; an Academy of Sculpture, and a Cabinet of Engravings and Drawings, formed under the direction of M. Krahe of Duffeldorff, in 400 folio volumes. - -

Of all thefe eftablifhments, none of the ornaments,

ornaments, or materials, that were portable, now remain at Manheim. The astronomical instruments, the celebrated collection of statues, the paintings and the prints have been removed, together with the Electoral treasure of diamonds and jewels, some to Munich and some to other places of security. But, though we missed a sight, which even its rarity would have rendered welcome, it seems proper, after such frequent notice of the barrenness of Germany, to mention what has been collected in one of its chief cities.

The expectation of an attack had dismantled other houses, besides the Elector's, of their furniture; for, in the Cour Palatine, a very spacious, and really a good inn, not a curtain and scarcely a spoon was left. *A cause de la guerre* was, indeed, the general excuse for every deficiency, used by those, who had civility enough to offer one; but, in truth, the war had not often incroached

croached upon the ordinary stock of conveniencies in Germany, which was previously too low to be capable of much reduction. The places, which the French had actually entered, are, of course, to be excepted; but it may otherwise be believed, that Germany can lose little by a war, more than the unfortunate labourers, whom it forces to become soldiers. The loss of wealth must come chiefly from other countries. A rich nation may give present treasure; a commercial nation may give both present treasure and the means of future competence.

The land near Manheim is chiefly planted with tobacco and madder, and the landscape is enlivened with small, but neat countryhouses, scattered along the margin of the Neckar. The neighbourhood abounds in pleasant rides, and, whether you wind the high banks of the majestic Rhine, or the borders of the more tranquil Neckar, the mountains of the Bergstraffe, tumbled upon

each

each other in wild confusion, generally form the magnificent back ground of the scene.

On returning from an excursion of this kind at the close of evening, the soldiers at the gates are frequently heard chanting martial songs in parts and chorus; a sonorous music in severe unison with the solemnity of the hour and the imperfect forms, that meet the eye, of sentinels keeping watch beneath the dusky gateways, while their brethren, reposing on the benches without, mingle their voices in the deep chorus. Rude and simple as are these strains, they are often singularly impressive, and touch the imagination with something approaching to horror, when the circumstances of the place are remembered, and it is considered how soon these men, sent to inflict death on others, may themselves be thrown into the unnumbered heap of the military slain.

SCHWETZ-

SCHWETZINGEN.

An excellent road, sheltered for nine English miles by rows of high poplars, conducted us through richly cultivated plains from Manheim to Schwetzingen, a small village, distinguished by an Electoral chateau and gardens. This was one of the pleasantest rides we had found in Germany, for the road, though it exhibited little of either the wild or picturesque, frequently opened towards the mountains, bright with a variety of colouring, and then again was shrouded among woods and plantations, that bordered the neighbouring fields, and brought faintly to remembrance the style and mingled verdure of our native landscape.

Schwetzingen had been very lately the Austrian head-quarters, for the army of the Upper

Upper Rhine, and some soldiers were still stationed near the road to guard an immense magazine of wood; but there were otherwise no military symptoms about the place.

The chateau is an old and inelegant building, not large enough to have been ever used as a formal residence. The present Elector has added to it two wings, each of six hundred feet long, but so low, that the apartments are all on the ground floor. Somewhat of that air of neglect, which can sadden even the most delightful scenes, is visible here; several of the windows are broken, and the theatre, music-room, and ball-room, which have been laid out in one of the wings, are abandoned to dust and lumber.

The gardens, however, are preserved in better order. Before the palace, a long vista of lawn and wood, with numerous and spacious fountains, guarded by statues, display something of the old French manner; other parts shew charming scenery, and deep sylvan recesses, where nature is again at liberty; in a bay formed by the woods is an amphitheatre of fragrant orange trees, placed in front of a light semicircular green-house, and crowned with lofty groves. Near this delicious spot, extends a bending arcade of lattice-work, interwoven with vines and many beautifully flowering plants; a sort of structure, the filagree lightness of which it is impossible not to admire, against precept, and perhaps, when general effect is considered, against necessary taste. In another part, sheltered by the woods, is an edifice in the style of a Turkish mosque, with its light cloistered courts, slender minarets, and painted entrances, inscribed with Arabic mottos, which by the German translations appear to express the pleasure of friendly conversation and of indolence in summer. The gardens have this result of a judicious arrangement, that they seem to extend much

beyond

beyond their real limits, which we discovered only by ascending one of the minarets. They are open to the public, during great part of every day, under certain rules for their preservation, of which copies are pasted up in several places.

CARLSRUHE.

At Schwetzingen the fine Electoral road concludes, and we began to wind along the skirts of a forest on the left, having on the right an open corn country, beyond which appeared the towers of Spires and Philipsburg, of which the former was then the head-quarters of the Austrian army, and the latter is memorable for having given birth to Melancthon in 1491. Waghausel and Bruchsal are small posting places in this route, at a village between which we had another instance of the little attention paid to travellers in Germany. At a small inn, noxious with some fumigation used against bugs, we were detained a quarter of an hour, because the landlord, who had gone out after our arrival, had not left word how much we should pay, and the poor old woman, who, without shoes or stockings, attended us, was terrified when we talked of leaving what was proper, and proceeding before his return.

About a mile beyond Bruchsal our postillion quitted the chauffée, and entered a summer road, through the deep and extensive forest of Carlsruhe, preserved by the Margrave of Baden for the shelter of game. Avenues cut through this forest for nine or ten miles in every direction, converge at his palace and city of Carlsruhe, as at a point. Other cruelties than those of the chase sometimes take place in these delightful scenes, for an amphitheatre has been formed in the woods, where imitations of a

Spanish

Spanish bull feast have been exhibited; to such horrid means of preventing vacuity of mind has a prince had recourse, who is otherwise distinguished for the elegance of his taste, and the suavity of his manners!

The scenery of this forest is very various. Sometimes we found our way through groves of ancient pine and fir, so thickly planted that their lower branches were withered for want of air, and it seemed as if the carriage could not proceed between them; at others we passed under the spreading shade of chesnuts, oak and walnut, and crossed many a cool stream, green with the impending foliage, on whose sequestered bank one almost expected to see the moralizing Jacques; so exactly did the scene accord with Shakespeare's description. The woods again opening, we found ourselves in a noble avenue, and saw the stag gracefully bounding across it "to more profound repose;" while now and then a hut, formed

of

of rude green planks under some old oak, seemed, by its smoked sides, to have often afforded a sheltered repast to hunting parties.

Near Carlsruhe the gardens of the Prince and then the palace become visible, the road winding along them, on the edge of the forest, till it enters the northern gate of the city, the uniformity of which has the same date as its completion, the ground plot having been entirely laid out between January and June 1715, on the 17th of which month the Margrave Charles William laid the foundation stone.

The streets are accordingly spacious, light, and exactly straight; but not so magnificent as those of Manheim, and still less enlivened with passengers. Since the commencement of the war, the gaieties of the Court, which afforded some occupation to the inhabitants, have ceased; the nobility have left their houses; and the Margrave is contented with the amufements of his library, in which Englifh literature is faid to fill a confiderable fpace.

Carlfruhe has the advantage of not being fortified; fo that the inhabitants are not oppreffed by a numerous garrifon, and ftrangers pafs through it, though fo near the feat of war, without interruption. It is lefs than Manheim by at leaft half, and has no confiderable public building, except the palace, from the fpacious area before which, all the ftreets proceed as *radii*, till their furtheft ends fill up the figure of a femicircle. The houfes in the area, which immediately front the palace, are built over a piazza interrupted only by the commencement of the ftreets. The palace has, of courfe, an unexampled advantage in the mixture of town and rural fcenery in its profpects, looking on one fide through all the ftreets of the city, and on the other through thirty-two foreft alleys, cut to various

rious lengths of from ten to fifteen English miles each; few, however, of the latter prospects are now commanded except from the upper windows, the present Elector having entirely changed the style of the intervening gardens, and permitted them to be laid out in the English taste, without respect to the thirty-two interfections, that rendered them conformable with the forest.

We passed part of two days at Carlsruhe, and were chiefly in these gardens, which are of the most enchanting beauty and richness. The warmth of the climate draws up colours for the shrubs and plants, which we thought could not be equalled in more northern latitudes; two thousand and seven hundred orange and lemon trees, loaded with fruit and blossoms, perfumed the air; and choice shrubs, marked with the Linnean distinctions, composed the thickets. The gardens, being limited only by the forests, appear to unite with them; and the

deep

deep verdure and luxuriance of the latter are contrasted sweetly with the tender green of the lawns and plants, and with the variety of scarce and majestic trees, mingled with the garden groves.

The palace is a large and sumptuous, though not an elegant edifice, built of stone like all the rest of the city, and at the same period. The Margrave generally resides in it, and has rendered it a valuable home, by adding greatly to the library, filling an observatory with excellent instruments, and preserving the whole structure in a condition not usual in Germany. The spot, compared with the surrounding country, appeared like Milton's Eden—like Paradise opened in the wild.

Beyond Carlsruhe the road begins to approach the Rhine, which we had lost sight of near Manheim; and, though the river is never within view, the country is considered as a military frontier, being constantly

patrolled

patrolled by troops. Some of these were of the Prince of Condé's army of emigrants, who have no uniform, and are distinguished only by the white cockade, and by a bandage of white linen, impressed with black *fleurs de lis*, upon the right arm. They were chiefly on foot, and then wore only their swords, without fire-arms.

Near the road, a small party of Austrians were guarding a magazine, before a tent, marked, like their regimentals, with green upon white. Soon afterwards, our postillion drew up on one side, to permit a train of carriages to pass, and immediately announced the *Prinz von Condé*, who was in an open landau, followed by two covered waggons for his kitchen and laundry, and by a coach with attendants.

He appeared to be between fifty and sixty; tall, not corpulent, and of an air, which might have announced the French courtier, if his rank had been unknown.

A star

A ſtar was embroidered upon his military ſurtout, but he had no guards, though travelling within the juriſdiction allotted to him as a general officer. So little was the road frequented at this period, that his was the ſecond or third carriage we had met, except military waggons, ſince leaving Mentz; a diſtance of more than eighty Engliſh miles.

The road for the whole ſtage between Carlſruhe and Raſtadt, about fifteen miles, is planted, as ſeems cuſtomary in Germany between the palaces of ſovereigns, with lofty trees, of which the ſhade was extremely refreſhing at this ſeaſon; the clouds of ſand, that roſe from the road, would otherwiſe have made the heat intolerable.

The firſt houſe in Raſtadt is the palace of the Margrave of Baden Baden, brother of the Margrave of Baden Durlach, whoſe reſidence is at Carlſruhe, a ſmall and heavy building, that fronts the avenue, and is

ſurrounded

surrounded with stone walls. The interior is said to be splendidly decorated, and a chamber is preserved in the state, in which Prince Eugene and Marshal Villars left it in 1714, after concluding the peace between the Emperor and Louis the Fourteenth. The Prince of Baden, being then a general in the service of the Emperor, had not been able to escape the vengeance of Louis, whose troops in 1688 first plundered, and then burnt, the palace and city, and in the war of the Succession they had a camp on the adjoining plain. The Prince is therefore supposed to have lent the palace, which he had rebuilt, with the more readiness, that the Marshal might see how perfectly he could overcome his loss. The plunder of the city in 1688 had continued for five days, and it is mentioned in its history that the French carried away fifteen waggon loads of wine of the vintage of 1572.

Rastadt, like Carlsruhe, is built upon one plan,

plan, but is as inferior to it in beauty, as in size. The chief street is, however, uncommonly broad, so much so, that the upper end is used as a market-place, and the statue of the founder, Prince Louis, in the centre, is seen with all the advantages of space and perspective. There is, notwithstanding, little appearance of traffic, and the inhabitants seemed to be much less numerous than the emigrant corps, which was then stationed there, the head quarters of the Prince of Condé being established in the city. We passed an hour at an inn, which was nearly filled by part of this corps, and were compelled to witness the distress and disappointment, excited by intelligence just then received of the state of affairs in the Low Countries.

A small park of artillery was kept on the southern side of Rastadt, where there is a handsome stone bridge over the river Murg, that falls into the Rhine, at the distance of a league from the city. Soon after, the road paſſes by the groves of the *Favorita*, a ſummer palace built by a dowager Margravine. We now drew nearer to the mountains of the Bergſtraſſe, which had diſappeared near Schwetzingen, and had riſen again partially through the morning miſts, ſoon after our quitting Carlſruhe. They are here of more awful height, and abrupt ſteepneſs than in the neighbourhood of Manheim, and, on their pointed brows, are frequently the ruins of caſtles, placed ſometimes where it ſeems as if no human foot could climb. The nearer we approached theſe mountains the more we had occaſion to admire the various tints of their granites. Sometimes the precipices were of a faint pink, then of a deep red, a dull purple, or a bluſh approaching to lilac, and ſometimes gleams of a pale yellow mingled with the low ſhrubs, that grew upon their ſides. The day was cloudleſs and bright, and we were

were too near thefe heights to be deceived by the illufions of aerial colouring; the real hues of their features were as beautiful, as their magnitude was fublime. The plains, that extend along their feet to the Rhine, are richly cultivated with corn, and, beyond the river, others, which appear to be equally fruitful, fpread towards the mountains of Alface, a correfponding chain with the Bergftraffe, vaft and now blue with diftance.

The manners of the people from Manheim downwards, are more civilized than in the upper parts of Germany; an improvement, which may with great probability be imputed to the fuperior fruitfulnefs of the country, that amends their condition, and with it the focial qualities. The farms are more numerous, the labourers lefs dejected, and the women, who ftill work barefooted in the fields, have fomewhat of a ruddy brown in their complexion, inftead of the fallownefs, that renders the ferocious, or fullen sullen air of the others more striking. They are also better dressed; for, though they retain the slouched woollen hat, they have caps; and towards the borders of Switzerland their appearance becomes picturesque. Here they frequently wear a blue petticoat with a cherry-coloured boddice, full white sleeves fastened above the elbow, and a muslin handkerchief thrown gracefully round the neck in a sort of roll; the hair sometimes platted round the head, and held on the crown with a large bodkin. On holidays, the girls have often a flat straw hat, with bows of ribband hanging behind. Higher up, the women wear their long black hair platted, but falling in a queue down the back.

The cottages are also somewhat better, and the sides entirely covered with vines, on which, in the beginning of July, were grapes bigger than capers, and in immense quantities. Sometimes Turkey corn is put

to

to dry under the projections of the firſt floor, and the gardens are ornamented with a ſhort alley of hops. Meat is however bad and ſcarce; the appearance ſo difguſting before it is dreſſed, that thoſe, who can accommodate their palates to the cooking, muſt endeavour to forget what they have ſeen. Butter is ſtill more ſcarce, and the little cheeſe that appears, is only a new white curd, made up in rolls, ſcarcely bigger than an egg. A ſort of beer is here made for ſervants, the taſte of which affords no ſymptom of either malt or hops; it is often nearly white, and appears to have been brewed but a few hours; what is ſomewhat browner is bottled, and ſold at about three-pence a quart.

Our road, this day, was ſeldom more than two leagues diſtant from the Rhine, and we expected to have heard the fire, which the Auſtrian and French poſts, who have their batteries on the two banks of the river,

river, frequently exchange with each other. The tranquillity was, however, as found as in any other country, and nothing but the continuance of patroles, and convoys reminded us of our nearness to the war. The peasants were as leisurely cutting their harvest, and all the other business of rural life was proceeding as uninterruptedly, as if there was no possibility of an attack. Yet we afterwards learned, that the French had, very early on the morning of this day, ineffectually attempted the passage of the Rhine, about fifteen miles higher up; and the firing had been distinctly heard at a little village where we dined.

One road, as short as this, lies immediately upon the margin of the river; and, as we were assured that none but military parties were fired at, we wished to pass it, for the purpose of observing the ingenious methods, by which a country so circumstanced is defended; but our postillion, who dreaded,

dreaded, that he might be preffed by the Auftrians, for the intrufion, refufed to venture upon it, and, inftead of proceeding to Kehl, which is directly oppofite to Strafbourg, we took the road for Offenburg, about three leagues from the Rhine.

The country through which our route now lay, better as it is than more northern parts, has fuffered fome pofitive injuries by the war. Before this, all the little towns, from Carlfruhe downwards, maintained fome commerce with France, on their own account, and fupplied carriage for that of others. In return for provifions and coarfe commodities for manufacture, carried to Strafbourg, they received the filks and woollens of France, to be difperfed at Franckfort, or Manheim. The intercourfe between the two countries was fo frequent, that nearly all the tradefmen, and many of the labouring perfons in this part of Germany fpeak a little French. The landlord of the house, where we dined, assured us that, though his village was so small, he had sufficient business before the war; now he was upon the point of removing to Offenburg, being unable to pay his rent, during the interruption of travelling.

A little before sun-set, we came to Appenweyer, one of these towns, from the entrance of which the spires of Strasbourg were so plainly visible that we could see the fanes glittering against the light, and even the forms of the fortifications near the water could be traced. In the midst of the straggling town of Appenweyer the loud sounds of martial music and then the appearance of troops, entering at the opposite end, surprised us. This was the advanced guard of several Austrian regiments, on their march to re-inforce the allied army in the Low Countries. Our postillion had drawn up, to surrender as much of the road as possible to them, but their march was so
irregular,

irregular, that they frequently thronged round the carriage; affording us sufficient opportunity to obferve how far their air correfponded with what has been fo often faid of the Auftrian foldiery.

Except as to their drefs and arms, their appearance is not military, according to any notion, which an Englifhman is likely to have formed; that is, there is nothing of activity, nothing of fpirit, of cheerfulnefs, of the correctnefs of difcipline, or of the eagernefs of the youthful in it. There is much of ferocity, much of timid cruelty, of fullennefs, indolence and awkwardnefs. They drefs up their faces with muftachios, and feem extremely defirous to imprefs terror. How far this may be effectual againft other troops we cannot know; but they certainly are, by their ferocious manners, and by the traits, which a nearer view of them difclofes, very terrible to the peaceful traveller.—Though now immediately under

the

the eyes of their officers they could scarcely refrain from petty insults, and from wishfully laying their hands upon our baggage.

About a thousand men passed in two divisions, which had commenced their march a few hours before, for the purpose of avoiding the heat of the day. As we proceeded, the trodden corn in the fields shewed where they had rested.

It was night before we reached Offenburg, where we were compelled to lodge at a wretched inn called the Post-house, the master of the other having that day removed to admit a new tenant; but the condition of the lodging was of little importance, for, all night, the heavy trampling of feet along the road below prevented sleep, and with the first dawn the sound of martial music drew us to the windows. It seemed like a dream, when the Austrian bands played *ça ira*, with double drums, and cymbals thrown almost up to our casements,

ments, louder than any we had ever heard before. This was the main body of the army, of which we had met the advanced party. Each regiment was followed by a long train of baggage carriages, of various and curious defcriptions, fome of the cabriolets having a woman nearly in man's apparel in the front, and behind, a large bafket higher than the carriage, filled with hay. This " tide of human exiftence" continued to pafs for feveral hours. But the whole army did not confift of more than three regiments of infantry, among which were thofe of D'Arcy, and Pellegrini, and one of horfe; for each of the Auftrian regiments of foot contains, when complete, two thoufand three hundred men. They had with them a fmall train of artillery, and were to proceed to the Low Countries as quick as they could march; but, fo uniform are the expedients of the councils of Vienna, that the opportunity of carrying thefe troops

troops down the Rhine in barges from Phillipſburg, where it was practicable, was not adopted, though this method would have ſaved two weeks out of three, and have landed the army unfatigued at its poſt.

All their regimentals were white, faced either with light blue, or pompadour, and ſeemed unſuitably delicate for figures ſo large and heavy. The cavalry were loaded with many articles of baggage, but their horſes appeared to be of the ſtrongeſt and moſt ſerviceable kind. This was a grand military ſhow, which it was impoſſible to ſee without many reflections on human nature and human miſery.

Offenburg is a ſmall town, in the Margraviate of Baden Baden, pleaſantly ſeated at the feet of the Bergſtraſſe, which the road again approaches ſo near as to be ſomewhat obſtructed by its acclivities. Our way lay along the baſe of theſe ſteeps, during the whole

whole day; and as we drew nearer to Switzerland, their height became ſtill more ſtupendous, and the mountains of Alſace ſeemed advancing to meet them in the long perſpective; the plains between, through which the Rhine gleamed in long ſweeps, appeared to be entirely covered with corn, and in the nearer ſcene joyous groups were loading the waggons with the harveſt. An harveſt of another kind was ripening among the lower rocks of the Bergſtraſſe, where the light green of the vines enlivened every cliff, and ſometimes overſpread the ruinous walls of what had once been fortreſſes.

We paſſed many villages, ſhaded with noble trees, which had more appearance of comfort than any we had ſeen, and which were enviable for the pleaſantneſs of their ſituation; their ſpacious ſtreet generally opening to the grandeur of the mountain viſta, that extended to the ſouth. In theſe landſcapes the peaſant girl, in the ſimple
dreſs

dress of the country, and balancing on her large straw hat an harvest keg, was a very picturesque figure.

It was evening when we came within view of Friburg, the last city of Germany on the borders of Switzerland, and found ourselves among mountains, which partook of the immensity and sublimity of those of that enchanting country. But what was our emotion, when, from an eminence, we discovered the pointed summits of what we believed to be the Swiss mountains themselves, a multitudinous assemblage rolled in the far-distant prospect! This glimpse of a country of all others in Europe the most astonishing and grand, awakened a thousand interesting recollections and delightful expectations; while we watched with regret even this partial vision vanishing from our eyes as we descended towards Friburg. The mountains, that encompass this city, have so much the character of the great,

that

that we immediately recollect the line of separation between Germany and Switzerland to be merely artificial, not marked even by a river. Yet while we yield to the awful pleasure which this eternal vastness inspires, we feel the insignificance of our temporary nature, and, seeming more than ever conscious by what a slender system our existence is upheld, somewhat of dejection and anxiety mingle with our admiration.

END OF THE FIRST VOLUME.

www.ingramcontent.com/pod-product-compliance
Lightning Source LLC
Chambersburg PA
CBHW051844300426
44117CB00006B/264